BLESSED WITHIN

Viral Plagues of inequality

BETTY C DUDNEY M.T.

WESTBOW
PRESS®
A DIVISION OF THOMAS NELSON
& ZONDERVAN

This book is a work of non-fiction. Unless otherwise noted, the author and the publisher make no explicit guarantees as to the accuracy of the information contained in this book and in some cases, names of people and places have been altered to protect their privacy.

WestBow Press books may be ordered through booksellers or by contacting:

WestBow Press
A Division of Thomas Nelson & Zondervan
1663 Liberty Drive
Bloomington, IN 47403
www.westbowpress.com
844-714-3454

Scripture quotations taken from The Holy Bible, New International Version® NIV® Copyright © 1973 1978 1984 2011 by Biblica, Inc. TM. Used by permission. All rights reserved worldwide.

ISBN: 978-1-6642-1027-1 (sc)
ISBN: 978-1-6642-1028-8 (e)

Library of Congress Control Number: 2020921031

Print information available on the last page.

WestBow Press rev. date: 01/18/2021

The design and name of this book cover, came in a Godly dream, just before waking on a Christmas morning, "BLESSED WITHIN", as well as most of the inspiration from experiences I have had in my long life with God's Holy Spirit. Very few supernatural experiences but each one shaped my life from seeing God's Hand at five years old, not another sign for over 25 years when I had a Spiritual Rebirth. Given only one word to share "Equality".

Except during a few years of intellectual doubt have just like most Christian believers felt the spiritual warmth of God's presence and been able to ask and receive answers in my mind that are always better than my own kind of thinking is!

To share the ways I've found that will work for you too, is my purpose for writing and has taken most of my life's time and energy what is now needed for a better world.

OUR ECONOMIC EXPLOITATION

The poverty of many people in our world does not point only to our personal efforts but to the economic exploitation of our unequal distribution systems, the misuse or unfair use of the world's resources.

Some want to not claim any responsibility for ancestors long gone. Yet everyone wants to receive as much as has been passed on to them and do not see this as a contradiction!

The message of the Universal Golden Rule is part of our Godly Created Spiritual nature to want to be equally or fairly treated. Hearts that have been too hurt or damaged will doubt.

WHAT'S IT'S ALL ABOUT?

To help prevent much of what is happening in our world and so much worse, such as the tampering with the DNA of our food seeds. Part of the Economic injustice as the most harming of the world's exploitation! In this most critical time in our history, not to do what we can will bring down eternal judgement on all, as well as 99% slavery and destruction to ourselves and those we love. We are chosen in this time and place, and gifted to be Godly Hands.

Learn by taking a lesson from these times to be conscious more than just indulging in your normal comfortable state in such a dangerous world, leaving the rest for someone else to do! Like knowing about the feminine half of God!

From inspired Words from God, written in Hebrew translated after many years, into Patriarchal languages created by males using only male names for God, like "Father", pronouns of "He, His, Him", leaving out the female, the Mother half of God's Image! Led us into a false Image of God (idolatry)! Yet our oldest Samarian Texts, and earliest Hebrew* Creation Stories tell us, "both male and female Created in God's Image". * *Genesis 1:27; 5:1.

The Parable of the first people, Adam and Eve, the first Biblical Prophecy of a coming Messiah, is a parable story written by a prophet Ahab I, who later became King Ahab I, with wife named Jezebel. Men's customs then of inequality became more than just primitive beliefs of 'physical might makes right'. Later they hid the female half of God by patriarchal masculine language's so people tended to think of God as being like only a male! The Universal Golden Rule message is the same found in God's Word of Equity, or "Equality" given at my Spiritual "Rebirth" as had been given ten years before, in1965, at Vatican II. Meaning Equal Rights, Respect and Equal Opportunity for both male and female, as well as racial equality, an end to discriminations.

So, needed because inequality causes much violence, wars resulting in poverty for many. Plus, over 50% of the world now making less than $3.day, starvation wages! Even those with good wages need only one family disaster, or one big health issue to wipe out a lifetime of savings. Less than 2% Corporate Owners unfairly control over 90% of world's economy by keeping excess profits, stocks, bonds, high interest, usury, paying many millions for CEO's to squeeze ever more from the workers, and products!

Our more cooperative female half are needed to balance the more aggressive male nature. To prevent a nuclear war on the horizon, that could send us back into the dark ages. At the end of this book is a copy single page of The Prophecy of "Equality" if given to 3, and each one gives to 3 more, in 15 cycles you can reach over 2 million! If you try send the first three to leaders such as The Pope, or your own Leaders.

Above all learn many reasons not to support inequality"!

CONTENTS

Contents

FOR BLESSINGS WITHIN

Blessings flow freely within, as well as without, when Equal Rights, Equal Concern, Equality rules our hearts instead of inequality!

To help us stop the idolatry of a male/only false Image of god, being used by the spirit of evil to justify aggression and violence, by the false belief that 'might makes right', to keep us in one war after another, and now close to a Nuclear World War III. If that were not enough, I can give you evidence for a tampering with our food supply. Natural food seeds given for the benefit of all now being owned, patented, by the 1% controlled Corporations to alter the DNA of food seeds with GMO's (genetically modified Organisms) using toxic, carcinogenic chemicals to control health and to increase cost, availability of food.

Changing the DNA of the seeds being grown in the fields and can make sterile the natural seeds sown anywhere nearby, as well as control profits that rightfully belong to all the people. Food not meant for just the profit of a few!

I repeat, when these altered GMO seeds are grown near natural or organic crops they can make natural seeds sterile, as a way to control not only profits but people's health and able to decrease population for easier control, to a few million or less, compared to our now billions, by being able to own the seeds price and add what they wish to change the DNA.

Already these GMO's have been put into some commercial foods, in corn syrups and other corn fillers and unknowingly used by many buying prepared dishes.

This may be our last few years to Stop supporting unjust economic inequality. One way is to let your Representatives know.

The present economic imbalance in political positions of power are held by a handful, owning controlling shares of many International Corporate boards. Less than 1% known to be in control of up to 90% of World's economy, natural resources!

Natural resources like the best within us, are meant for the benefit of all. They have much power, but the people's Power of knowing, is what they fear. So, don't keep it a secret. God favors people's equal rights and will help when asked.

Religious leaders who continue to practice discrimination, inequality for the female half, are allowing inequality to be justified in those who continue to profit from sinful 'Usury' and other profits primarily for more power. Stop supporting wherever you can, the practice of inequality, like excess interest rates for the use of money.

Our Peace and Goodwill comes first from practicing the Golden Rule of treating others with equal fairness and with equal rights. War, revenge, comes when we do less.

This Prophecy of "Equality" not been given just to me! Given at Vatican II, in Article 29, Pastoral Constitution, 1965 "to end racial, sexual discrimination, as not the Will of God".

This about once in a hundred years council by Bishops, usually becomes The Canon law of the Church except the first Pope John Paul I to consider it, after

100 Religious Sisters came to Rome to appeal to Him, was found dead, three days later.

None since have any been so brave about our inequality until this last Pope Francis. But each of us sooner or later, are judged in this life or the next, by both the good we have done or failed to do.

The third time of my seeing God's Hand, discouraged I had tried to walk away, after tiring of trying to witness to The Catholic Church and got less than a block away when didn't see, but strongly felt, God's Hand in my own.

Looking down to try to see what obviously I was feeling with no one else near me, strongly felt God's Hand in mine spin me around in my tracks. Knowing then not to ever try to leave again but did start trying to write about it for the next 25 years.

By staying, I learned while the world is still in the slavery of sin by the Grace of a Godly Love, all of us can be set free in our Spirit. The already given sacrifice of Christ, for all who are willing to follow the guidance of the Holy Spirit living in your heart, first ask for any needed forgiveness of past sins and allow the Holy Spirit in to comfort, guide you to the fullness of Truth!

To be Free, those who chose to allow God's Holy Spirit to confirm what you know to do while being led to eternal life after this short one on earth.

John, one of Jesus closest friends, followers, and maybe a converted Priest wrote: "God is Love. Whoever lives in love lives in God, and God in them." *I John 4:16 Vs.17 goes on to say, especially for us today "For God did not send his Son into the world to condemn the world, but to save the world through Him." Everyone who does evil hates that light and will not come in for fear that their deeds will be exposed."

Over 22 references to who God is in Bible. The first in Deut. 6:4 "Hear, O Israel: The Lord our God, the Lord is One. In John 1:18 No one has ever seen God, (all of God) but God the One and Only Son, who is at "ABBA's" side, Jesus has made him known.

The last reference of who God is, in Rev. 4:8 "Holy, holy, holy is the Lord God Almighty, who was, and is, and is to come."

Jesus called God, "ABBA", meaning "Heavenly Parent". From the Aramaic language of the people Jesus taught includes the Mother as well as the Father Image as literally meaning our "Heavenly Parent". AB=Dad, BA=Mom, combined becomes "ABBA".

God as "One" in Spirit can and includes the Image of a Holy Family like our human families, as a Father/Mother/Child kind of family.

In the first Biblical chapter of Genesis 1:27 we are told God created both male and female in the Image of God and this is repeated in chapter 5:1, official creation stories of Priest.

A Parable, not a literal story but meant to represent the first people, called Adam and Eve, later added in between the two original Creation stories, that say God created both male and female in the Image of God. Not the same story of creation. A Parable that was only meant to explain how the sin of listening to evil instead of God, lost both male and female the Paradise for them God had created, by the first people choosing to believe an evil snake over God's warning it would kill them (Spiritually). The parable story was to give hope of an eventual Messiah who could stop the spirit of evil in the world, by spiritual belief.

The prophet Ahab I, who later became A King in Samaria, got addicted to riches and power, married an evil Jezebel who had a man killed because he wouldn't give or sell cheap his land to the King. Jezebel is also famous for trying to kill one of the great prophets Elijah and met a terrible death, he lost all his future Sons and only remembered as the husband of Jezebel. He is also the one who introduced the parable that helped justify the sexist inequality of his time.

One or two or more, thousands of years passed, no one knows how long, but a long time before anyone would see God's Hand again, the Jewish people who turned to a Loving God, found themselves enslaved to the Egyptians while living there as the Jewish people grew in strength. The Pharaoh had babies under two killed to keep their population down. When the Jewish people asked God to save them, they were sent the then elderly shepherd Moses, who miraculously lead them across the Red Sea and into the desert towards what was promised, a land of milk and honey. During this time God forbid them to worship any created image, human or animal, only The Spirit of God, by giving Moses the 10 Commandments.

For many years they would be faithful then slowly begin to worship and follow other traditions or false Images of God and become spiritually weak and then be conquered by stronger nations.

Finally, The Messiah was born to them but their leaders in their pride did not recognize Jesus as the people's Redeemer, Preacher and Healer and in fear of the people following him instead of them, they had crucified him on a Cross. Three days later he arose from the Dead and spent 40 days among the people, before he was seen by many ascending into the Heavens. This is the Christian belief I was raised in. Just as Moses, Daniel and others, have seen God's Hand in history. I once counted over 500 times where God's Hand is mentioned in the Bible. Actual being seen, or more common as a symbol of God coming into the world to act.

Three times I have actually experienced God's Hand. First over 80 years ago, in the same month Adolph Hitler became President, to start world War II. The second time, not for 25 years later, given the one Word of "Equality", I believe to help stop a nuclear World War III that we are still headed for that could put us all back into the stone age.

Having experienced these truths for so many years can only conclude that God is our Heavenly Mother as well as Father. For what is the meaning of a Father without a Mother?

Have also learned that physically we are both male and female, created in God's Image, and share the same sexual hormones, bones, organs, etc. Male and female with both, just more of one than the other of the two primary sexual hormones when in different reproductive stages of life for both sexes. Sexual organs, some out, some in, to copulate. The female's sexual organ being inside, ending in the womb.

Accepting a false or male only Image of God allows evil in your heart and hardens it, and why this sin of idolatry is able to at least partly control your thoughts and actions, working against people's best interest for Peace and belief in an equally Loving God.

If you are into that sin and most of us have been to some extent in our life just by our worldly conditionings, there is a way to confirm for yourself but only if you first can and want to free your mind from any negative or ungodly preconceived images!

God's Holy Spirit is A Spirit of Holy Love, a God of Equity, equally for all, and "is not a god of partiality" * Deuteronomy.10:17; Acts: 10:34; Romans 2:11; Gal.3:28.

We were Created for Good, not as slaves of evil. 'Those who have more, much more is expected.'

We have a created need to be spiritually "reborn", as well as physically reborn, where The Holy Spirit of God comes to live in our hearts. Jesus declared, "I tell you the truth, no one can see all the kingdom of God unless he is born again. * *See how in John 3:3-8; Acts1:4,5

Only way to really free yourself from the control of a male created or male image of god, used by evil to justify the aggression and violence or 'might makes right', that fights to rule in our physical world, and has a lot of control in the way of thinking, in hurting, controlled by ignorance and with unloving hearts.

Determined to keep us by nature violent, keeping us in one war after another, and now near a Nuclear World War III. That could put us back in the dark ages.

To not be caught up by evil is to be able to give your honest sincere Thanks for a Creator, The Holy Spirit of Love, not bound by gender, recognized as being beyond our physical and limiting matter, time or space. Who can live within us, in our Physical Realm yet not limited as we are in this physical life like we must sometimes even daily choose who we bow to? By Free Will Choice we can accept and place our faith in a Loving Creator, in the guidance of God's Holy Spirit or we will tend to Crown Ourselves or others as the sole judge, by whatever whoever seems most logical or valid at the time!

The beliefs of inequality we have all been indoctrinated into. In translating the original languages, by changing the meaning of "ABBA" to just "Father" of our now Patriarchal languages, though theologically still known to include the Mother or feminine half, is not in laymen's terms known to have a feminine nature.

When questions come up often just excused or taught as God has no gender, but while still using human male nouns and pronouns of He, His! Creating for many the sin of idolatry. The worship of a male/only image of God for most from childhood on!

Perpetuating not only a lower respect or concern, as well as a lower pay scale, for the female half.

Continuing to justify beliefs of inequality that also includes males, for all workers, as somehow less than those with higher incomes, while the lowest cost of labor, products, are used to increase the profits of those based on investments, ownership of land and property, previously taken by force in wars of a stronger group or nation.

Since it is the labor and time of the workers, male or female, as well as the investors, that make the profits, should not the profits be more equally shared, especially in times of Peace?

Even here in the U.S., the majority of workers are making only a minimum wage, barely enough for one to live on, or to keep up with, the always increasing higher cost of living! While most profits are going primarily to the top less than 2%-10%. Still most here in America are doing better than most others in the world, where children are forced into the labor force as early as 5 or 6 years old, or starve, about half not yet able to go to school long enough to develop any potential talents, that invariably would be better for us all!

This is not right, when the top few families have more than the total income of 90% of the rest of many millions! In Country after Country and worse in third world countries! The best and fastest Cure is to become Spiritually mature. By first asking God's Help to confirm for yourself with a Spiritual "Rebirth", necessary for God's Spirit to help you be connected to a God who loves each one equally, instead of being deceived by an evil spirit.

God's Holy Spirit gives special gifts to help you know what is best for you, as well as others! The Book of Romans in 8:28 tells us God can cause Good to work together for the good of all those willing to Love such a God, and to Love One Another, can even turn enemies into friends!

"And we know that in all things God works for the good of those who Love Him to bring about what is good." When Spiritually Reborn, we grow in our understanding of a God of Love who can live within our hearts and give hope of eternal life. Jesus taught about in Gospel of John 3:3-7

The Jesus Way, to Love One Another is the Sum of The Laws and Prophets, even to love your enemies, as a possible way to make them friends, instead of your enemies! Allowing God into your heart in seeking The Holy Spirit guidance is the best way, no matter the darkness around you, keep on in God's Goodness and the Christ light!

Those given more, much more is expected from them! Not only to share of themselves and with each other, we are to share until the basic needs of All have been met. Few of us have done as much as we can.

A much more worthy way of living, whether you believe there is an afterlife or not. For less, in the long run, leaves you with less. Life feels better when we live up to our very best! Most in other beliefs are also expected to live up to the Universal known Message from God, of the Golden Rule to treat others as you would most want to be treated. Much like the prophecy of "Equality". Herein lies the potential of achieving Heaven, not only after this life, but in the now, for those willing to practice such a Holy Love! To see, do this, you need the help of God's Holy Spirit, as our Heavenly Spiritual Parent. Who like a Spiritual midwife as our Mother, as well as like a Protective Father, are able to guide us into the fullness of Truth, but not without your free will!

We were not created or born to be robots. We must freely accept the Godly Way as being the better way, or we will tend to more selfish worldly ways! To keep our precious free-will ours. God does not normally interfere in our world, but sets for a later time, individual and worldly judgements, yet could come at any time for us when we are finally released from our earthly ties.

Spiritual-ness such a mystery cannot be easily proven, but then cannot be disproven. Accepted primarily in Faith, that our consciousness or soul continues after this human life. When not to believe is to be without much hope, never knowing when each breath could be our last!

Best to choose Hope, for a later or even now confirming moment of knowing. Many people can and have testified to! Worth hearing. Such as many times when you know you are doing God's Will, instead of just your own more selfish Will, can then often get one of God's way of confirmation. This you cannot get when you are just doing your own thing!

Or even while holding on to some of your own personal unforgiveness of yourself or others! Just doesn't work that way and pulls you into an opposite belief.

You won't necessary even be able to prove it to anyone else, when you do see the evidence, for it is something your soul and heart experiences! Yet few spend their life in certainty of anything. When you do find assurance, you will and should continue to Praise God in the knowing!

Selfishness and greed have convinced many in power today that they are the only ones that matter. Steeped in this belief of inequality, they can only see the world as just a 'dog eat dog world', where 'might makes right'. Some believe there is nothing beyond, physical matter is all there is!

The only proof that they are likely to accept, is what must miraculously be experienced for yourself. With great Signs and Wonders, Jesus said, is what it takes for most to believe! Miraculous signs and wonder come only when invited into the individual heart, where The Holy Spirit wants to be!

Find out for yourself, by getting to know the one who already knows all about you, who will tell you, in your own unique way all the evidence you will need, if you are willing to be cleansed by forgiving and by being forgiven in mind and spirit. Ask for the evidence, but first must start with a clear conscience.

For any negative unforgiveness or a need yet for forgiveness will keep you from fully spiritually "seeing or hearing".

Seek and keep asking in prayer, till you know you have received it. It took me two weeks of praying at every opportunity, after years of doubting. I began to realize maybe it was not God, but us humans, who were not doing such a good job of running our world. So, I started asking for an undeniable sign. By first asking God, to forgive me for everything I could think of, that I had ever done that was not right, before finally God did answer me. No matter how long it takes, it is worth it, to be convinced. You will know when you are prayed up enough, and free of any known sin.

Time is short for those of us here, and our individual eternity is at stake, as well as the state of our world. There is lots of Archeological evidence now, of other civilizations from thousands of years ago, who may actually have even blown themselves up, or been destroyed by others more than once. Our civilization has advanced to such great technology, it can blow itself up again, if continuing the beliefs of 'might makes right', and so much inequality, that seems to have sent more than one or similar civilizations back to the dark ages.

Much of my worldly interest has been the discoveries of Archeology, after learning the millions of years of our planet's age. We have evidence dug out of the ground of many civilizations recycling violent natures who allowed evil rather than a God of Love to guide.

We have a chance now to stop our loosing history and recurring cycles of inequality, violence, slavery! Yet needs to happen with the help of many Spiritually "Reborn" in God's Power and Strength! There are enough who do want to do the right thing, by using the guidance of God's Holy Spirit, we could turn our world and beliefs into a better, fairer, more just world, even for an potential eternal time of Peace if enough of us can control our negative physical nature with our more positive Spiritual nature.

If all you can do is pray, we will need those prayers, for there is power in prayer. Will be needed every day until inequality is ended and heaven found within us, as well as without. End times or Armageddon seem still hundreds or more years away, but not a World War III, counting the nukes in so many countries now, is at our doorstep, and what I thought was our next big world disaster this last year, until the Covid-19 Viral Plague began, then realized my Prophetic feeling of a world disaster was maybe not a war but this virus, that is having a world-wide affect, not seen in so many since the 1918 virus that hit much of the world then. As has many such Plagues in the past.

Some have been heard in big economic power positions, convinced the answer to most of the world's population is to eliminate as many as possible! So, a world war cannot yet be eliminated. I'll leave that for another. I'm satisfied with the Virus as the fulfillment of mine, a necessary alternative of a nuclear war, that would have been so much worse.

These few in such power positions, already have access to fortified cities in guarded mountains in the Alps, in U.S., and Down Under the known underground cities, some even connected, already dug out and manned. They do mean business, as they continue to profit highly from not only the making and selling of weapons, to both sides, to Terrorist as well as Dictators, resulted already in much conflict and death, destruction, causing much migration, poverty and fear. War has always created all kinds of destruction to families, community.

There are other plans to control people, more than most already are. For the first time actually being able to change the DNA of our food seeds, so not only the seeds have to be bought but are sterile after one season's use. While nearby Organic or natural seeds of a similar kind being grown, are made sterile too, by just the wind carrying the new GMO seeds into their nearby fields!

God created in the best possible way for the use of all, a basic right of life, from nature, we need to affirm, as we are our 'brother's keeper', or we put a curse on ourselves and others! How can there be a food or seed ownership? Allowing the forever altering of the DNA nature of our food? Making sterile any organic growing crops? With our now little or no legal regulations, for the few high contributing contribution funds to lawmakers, taken as needed for re-elections? Money contributions have to be limited, to keep us free and equal, for each one to have a vote!

In my growing up, feeling safe living here in America, we still heard about some of the atrocities of those who had started the Second World War, soon after it was happening. Often using prisoners, including children. One of my favorite Uncles, only 10 years older, flew over 50 missions before the end of WWII, shot down twice behind enemy lines, and came back with a German Lugar gun he had found in a tank with dead Germans inside, becoming an alcoholic when he returned, from what he had seen and caused others to suffer, felt he had had to do at the time.

Remember that the next time you see a homeless man or woman, maybe still shell shocked, mentally disturbed, sick from some personal or war related injury, of our survivors, the so-called war victors, who end up suffering the ungodly nature of war for the killing of others. Killing other humans, even in war is not normal, and leaves many kinds of scars, hard to heal.

Historically some have justified their wars, when successful as God Ordained, but God's Commandment from the beginning was not to kill each other, but to Love One Another, even our enemies. Yes, we have the right to defend, and we must defend ourselves and others who can't defend themselves, from those who try to take away anyone's right to life and liberty, even for the pursuit of happiness, our American Democratic Constitution reads. Yet we still need to realize and plan for the mental, emotional, physical consequences in any violent defense, for all involved. Just what we heard about in World War II, were enough to impress us of people's ungodly cruelty to each other in times of war.

Over the years I've seen so many, especially children, still being exposed to violence, some daily by adults, and in the movies, on TV, so many forms in the media, indoctrinations into violence. So important as children and as adults, most things in our lives are positive, and not negative. We need people and things to be thankful for, to be able to develop normally.

Give thanks to God for our next breath if nothing else, as we learn to go towards a positive way and away from a cycle of violence or bitterness!

Seems to be part of the present conditioning of the heart as well as the mind, to accept violence even bullying as part of life's belief of the inequality, as being a normal way, it is an evil. Doesn't have to be. Programs to stop bullying in schools do help, we have a few really excellent ones, we need so many more! In all forms of learning and media.

Today's so much playing of violent games, whether watching sports or video games. Maybe some help to release the many frustrations of life, we all tend to build up, but it seems more likely a cause of increasingly insensitivity to acts of violence, to be actually a stimulate and the acceptance of seemingly ever more violence, in most communities in our times now!

Shouldn't we be trying instead, to decrease everyone's exposure to so much violence? A job for all of us to do our part about, those who are aware of it. Who else if not us?

ProjectAwake.org is one such program I've seen here in Tennessee that blends special performing arts to connect with the needs of students and adults too, for a large room or gym. One of the many ways of knowing how much each life matters. Ways to protect. ProjectAwake.org is one worth checking into, especially during the high school years.

To know where best to spend extra time and energy you need the greater intelligence of God's Holy Spirit and guidance, so helpful to spend at least a little time in quiet meditation, or prayer on a daily first thing in the morning and/or evening. When possible to make a habit of at least one or the other, a few minuet's we could all spare and get in a habit of.

The third Biblical Chapter of John is one of the places in the Gospels that tell us about our need to have a Spiritual "Rebirth". There are many worthwhile reasons to have such a Holy Spirit Friend as God, who can help you be not only your best here, but lead you to an eternal life in Heaven, after this life!

Being Omnipresent, in all things God already knows your needs, but for you, to be able to know why and how, you will need to clear the slate so to speak, of a negative past.

To first even see the need, even want to communicate, not really until you are willing to be open to wanting a clean heart. To be able to begin each new day, recognizing this life is a Holy Gift, not to be taken for granted. Finding something to be thankful for in the having! Some of God's most precious children have learned about having such a gift, by finding themselves laid aside in sickbeds or shut away in prisons. Others have voluntarily learned the discipline and advantages of spending time alone with God's Holy Spirit.

The Holy Spirit, Jesus said would come as a Spirit within, to be able to guide all those willing to believe and follow a God of Holy Love. To "Love One Another" * "even your enemies", as the only way to be able to make them friends instead! *Matt 5:44; 7:12; Luke 6:27

UNGODLY EVIDENCE

Dear Pastor Dean,

We need to reach many people to use inclusive language and stop using Patriarchal languages with only male nouns and male pronouns for most anything in authority.

That is only one of the reasons I believe God gave me the Prophecy of "Equality" 10 years after Vatican II, when they failed to end discrimination, after The Holy Spirit quoted way back in 1965 as saying, "In The Church… there is to be no more discrimination as to race or sex…as not the will of God".

About two years later in 1975 I felt led to learn more about the Catholic Religion, trying to get well from an inoculation while working in our county Hospital, while taking blood on an Emergency call from a very sick man in delirium, who later died, as I almost did too as it turned out to be a deadly virus, that wrecking my immune system for at least 20 years.

God insisted I then go into The Church to be able to Witness to "Equality" and I agreed as it was something I could do.

Only in the past few months have been released from that commitment after their attempts to keep women from having equal rights campaigned illegally from Archbishops to Priest to elect Trump, by putting rights of fetus above the women's and already born rights. Allowing again males the right to control a woman's body without her consent.

Since Catholic means Universal Believer I still want to remain, not as a Roman Catholic but as a Christian Catholic, because the Roman Church seems to be now controlled at the top of their Hierarchy by many ultra conservatives who don't want to give up even part of their power, none of it to the female half they do or at the top know is God's Image too.

The rest don't seem to want to deal with the issue, some Christians prefer to say "Jesus is coming back just any day"! Forgetting that a day is like 1000 years with God, or more! Those of us able to talk and confirm things with the Holy Spirit seem few and far between, because most of us consciously or subconsciously, are into male idolatry of God as male because of the patriarchal languages. Even to the point of thinking the Holy Spirit is only male, at least most Theologians know it as a female word. Just looking at the ancient Hebrew and Aramaic letters, I got to see for myself in Elijah's Cave, a little down from the Top of Mt. Sinai in 1986. ('l best I can do on this computer), pronounced (EL), later changed to Elohim, to include the Trinity of Mother, Father, Child, as Family.

Thank You for having an open heart and not being into an idolatry that limits our ability to see and hear the Prophecy of "Equality".

Your friend "In Christ",

Pastor Dean, like many others I've met on the Internet know in their good hearts that Equality is better than inequality! But the power of inequality can be addictive, or like most things at least over time becomes a habit.

Very hard to have only Good Habits, but we have to keep trying, or we slip into troubles.

One of our most overlooked dangers that now threatens much of human life, is the gradual private takeover of our food seeds, the primary food supply. Not only in the Corporate profit side of farming but in their scientific ability in labs to modify the seeds DNA.

To create a better nutritious food given, but the bottom line of most Corporations has been for the sake of profits, for the owners, and much worse, as a way of controlling peoples not only for profits but even for mind control and slave workers.

These DNA changes are currently being done on little known Islands, like on one of the outer Hawaiian Islands where I felt a Godly need to go to, Kauai in Hawaii, and did when an elderly friend offered to rent me, for no more money than where I was then living in the middle of California, a private room and bath with a shared kitchen, with two others who had their own rooms, in a three bedroom apartment close to a bus stop. The day I got off the plane I had noticed, a large protesting group and soon joined them in a march to the city hall.

Hundreds of mostly younger people protesting against the five International Corporate farms there in the Islands and their labs. They had found out they were experimenting with known poisons, toxins, on and inside the growing food seeds to legally patent them in the US. Experimenting in labs with the changing of the DNA the natural seeds with GMO's = Genetically Engineered Organisms! Known to be carcinogenic, most toxic in some other ways too.

For many years starting heavily in the 40's and 50's, pesticides of very toxic, poisonous chemicals, have been used, first for weed and pest control, like 'Round up' I've used myself to control house pests, and used to increase the yields on many family farms. Now many of these farms are owned or being leased out by larger farm Corporations, joining with other International Corporations for more control of our world's economy, even many of our natural resources. Natural resources created and originally meant by God for the use of all.

On the Island of Kauai, they are adding and testing potential toxins to change the DNA of the food seeds, then growing in fields the seed beds for future crops!

Within the borders of the United States there are many fields of these DNA modified seeds, that have had very little or insufficient human testing, but already patented and being used for most of our US grown corn crops, outside of those being organically farmed.

Corn being used in the making of corn syrup. One of the most common fillers added to many kinds of processed foods, for taste and makes it cheaper to produce. Most people are unlikely to read or know the DNA source of the listed ingredients they buy and may not realize some may be from such modified ingredients, GMO's, Genetically Modified Organisms, unless they are specifically labeled.

Many are little tested for all kinds of possible things relating to our human safety, including some of the suspected cancer-causing substances, and many other kinds of added organisms, or chemicals in levels little known about, just how dangerous short or long-term use is, for at least some, more sensitive people. When done by adding to and/or changing the DNA within the natural seeds. Like trying to make improvements on Creation, more likely to have the opposite effect!

We have a whole generation of humans, unsigned up for and mostly unaware that they are being used as guinea pigs, let alone for hard to trace or track, substances for the direct or indirect effects on the human body, in new modified foods. Sold as a business, primarily for profits. Without sufficient moral concern for permanent and irreversible damage to everyone's food supply, as GMO seeds can make sterile similar Organic seeds grown nearby.

Chemicals added to the diet can act as carcinogens and could be why our cancer rate in the U.S. keeps going sky high and most developed countries in recent years, in the advanced countries using more of these GMO foods. I realize other factors too, but GMO food is a big one, as well as our necessity for clean water, the air we breathe.

We now seem to be faced with all kinds of pollutants that can affect health, even too many airplanes in the air dropping fuel pollutants, especially vulnerable are the young and elderly.

Little testing for safety of humans as is possible to get through the government requirements are being done at present, often overworked, understaffed and an ever-limited government budget. Even the hiring of recent former employees of the same companies where their products are being tested by the FDA the Federal Department of Agriculture! The agencies of the US government are closely tied, and allied at times, by at least several of the International Food Corporations who are investing, in the seed experimentation which seems to be a possible conflict of interest? Since such large Corporate Organizations are known for their large contributions to politicians on both sides of the political Isles.

Lobbies of both food and chemical corporations have also been encouraging the removal of as many regulations as possible, especially those that would cut into their profit base! As has our present 2020 Administration, and those they have appointed as Department Heads, who may already have, or are planning on investing for profits, in some of these same food and chemical Corporations?

Privately-owned modified seeds containing all kinds of foreign organisms GMO's, are not only a present ongoing threat, but an even greater threat to the world's future food supply.

Without sufficient government oversight, that we don't have at this point, and with few actual impartially controlled tests, because once the seeds are DNA altered, the changes may be irreversible. Companies like Monsanto, and Dow International, have faced little media coverage, as do most large National media's Corporations possibly because of their lobby and financial campaign influence, plus their media investments.

Have recently heard of private ongoing court battles with the chemical maker of Agent Orange, one of the causes affecting so many. Known to cause Parkinson like diseases, with a definite link to the pesticide chemical known as Agent Orange. Not to mention other Cancer-causing chemicals, responsible for a yearly increase, especially here in the states of young people with all kinds of possibly related allergic type bodily reactions, and even cancers.

At least some of the sick and homeless Veterans have turned to the use of alcohol and street drugs for lack of expensive prescription drugs to control or kill the pain from their sickness and exposure to chemicals like Agent Orange during its widespread use, and exposure while they served in Viet Nam.

Some of these same ingredients are still being used in yards for pest and weeds. 'Roundup' one of the most advertised in ads, is still being sold, as I write.

Also being used on many farm fields, on and around farm raised animals and food products we all then consume.

The GMO seeds being grown by seed companies are able to adversely affect our future world's food supply. Allow the big Corporate owners not only to be able to control the Price of food and its production, but what actually goes into the seeds, for good or ill.

It is those at the top of the world's moral, political, economic systems, those in the deciding and controlling positions, who tend to live such unequal, and separated kinds of living from the great majority, living lives of inequality and great privilege, who do not want to realize how much better and safer a world all of us could have, with the belief and practice of equal fairness and concern for others.

We are all interconnected and what affects one in some way affects others sooner or later. Those at the very top, continue to set the world's public moral examples, in not only words but in their actions or lack of.

The continuing of one war after another, by males in control unable to come to any kind of peaceful negotiations will not without the help of women in similar equal positions to help with the negotiations.

Along with the rapidly losing of the natural God quality of our food supply, that affects many of us directly, by what is happened already to food seeds.

Not to mention the unfair distribution of wealth from the 1% already controlling up to 90% of our economy, ideally at least half of that 90% should be benefiting all, not only the workers, but the consumers to who pay the extra unnecessary prices deserve to have basic safety nets for the ending of the starvation of children, and needed health care, as well as education for human rights, to develop the talents now being wasted.

Human safety nets, that are not now available, even in most of the industrialized nations, let along in third world countries. When seen, should be no longer acceptable and is curable by a fair, just taxation, would make life bearable for the poorest and stop the starvation and hunger, inexcusable for the whole top 2% to not be paying more of their share so all of us would be safer and the world a better place to be.

Food makes our very life blood, our physical life force. I learned this partly, from working many nights in Emergency Labs for over 17 years, in both County and other kinds of hospitals, and medical clinics. Mostly in emergency night work, cross-matching blood for accident victims, as well as doing many other blood and chemistry test.

Blood is gender neutral, just a few different types we have labeled A's, B's, and O's, mostly O's. In some races where one type of blood may be more prevalent, found more frequently, but not as far as sex, or same types for blood does not discriminate.

Those who think they can avoid such dangers of GMO's by using only Organic food maybe don't yet know, or haven't heard, that Sterile GMO's, the genetically modified organisms put within the seeds, also make sterile any similar Organic seeds grown in fields nearby, or where-ever winds or men, might carry the modified seeds. We, while here on earth are what we eat. Our health, human life depends now, on those who own or oversee the Company Store! As well as those who feed us our spiritual morality.

Isn't it time to make the Company store a Co-op of the People's food, owned by the People, for the people, and not for just a few who want to profit and control what our food is, or how much we can have! By whatever kind of population control they want to use it for?

We have a need to realize the kind of a Frankenstein plot that such god playing with the seeds that feeds our life blood can have, and to know there are players involved who are not there to work for everyone's common good, both in and out of the board rooms!

Could or should work towards a competition of two kinds of food distributions systems, one owned just by the People, democratically for the people. Would be nice to have a choice, not just in one town, but in most! Not have to continue to support those seeking primarily profits for only a few.

Good Organic food helps as much as one can afford, find or grow. Most of our food produced now is not technically very Organic. Most if not eating organically need to be taking supplements for best health. Keep active doing worthwhile work or play, moderation in most things, except for the things you know are not good for you in particular.

Our collective needs for a better world, are found even in our wilderness areas, as well as in the inner cities. Have learned from reading Archeological evidence and watching Nature TV shows, where the rising of oceans from climate changes have historically sunk coastal cities in the past. This is where so many of our world's populations prefer to live, and where so much international shipping and trade take place. Climate changes from whatever cause, still very much matter, when life gets back to normal travel! Maybe we will have all electric cars by then. Airplanes?

Spent most of what little extra money I have had, time and energy, trying to write for as many as possible, to share the knowledge God has given or allowed me to see over the years. Primarily the Word of "Equality", given during my Spiritual "Rebirth".

Between times I too struggled with the injustice and unfairness, sometimes blaming God for not interfering with the misuse of human free will, until learning our life here is our spiritual growth or loss, by our choice or use, of each one's limited free will. It is God's Better Will that does rarely intercede, always impartially to preserve God's better plan Be willing to help not hinder.

"Come to me, all you who are weary and burdened, and I will give you rest. Take my yoke upon you and learn from me, for I am gentle and humble of heart, and you will find rest for your souls. For my yoke is easy, and my burden light." * Mt.11:28-30; John 13:15

Jesus repeating what the Prophet Jeremiah had said in Jer.6:16 "This is what the Lord says" Stand at the Crossroads and look, ask for the ancient paths, ask where the good way is and walk in it. Ps.119:3 And you will find rest for your souls. Matt. 11:29 But you said 'we will not walk in it...Jer. 6:18 Therefore hear, O nations; observe, O witnesses, what will happen to them. Hear O Earth Is.1:2: Jer. 22:29 I Am bringing disaster on the people.

Joshua 23:15 the fruit of their selfishness, because they have not listened to My Words and have rejected My Laws. Only later in Jeremiah does God say, "Reform your ways and your actions, and I will let you live in this place." Jer. 7:3-5 if you really change your ways and your actions and deal with each other Justly. Vs.6 if you do not follow other gods to your own harm. Vs.9 "Will you steal and murder, commit Adultery and Perjury, burn incense to Baals (a male only god) But I have been watching! Declares the Lord."

To enter Heaven here or there, we need the "Spiritual Rebirth" of John 3:3, to be able to be guided to, or to see the fullness of Truth. I know from experience how much we need this Spiritual Rebirth, from experiencing negative Spiritual beings, as well as those who think of themselves as Human gods and believers of inequality. They do what they can to control, manipulate others to do their will, rather than God's ways of each ones free will, ideal in the freedoms of Democracy or just goodwill towards others. How long this continues or if it is allowed to get worse, depends at least partly on those of us who happen to be living in our days, by what we do or fail to do!

Hopefully by choosing to work with God, for ourselves and those in our world, we may feel at least some responsibility for, as our human brothers and sisters, children of God.

Our efforts may or may not make a difference now, but it has in the past, and no reason why it can't again.

Just know we have a God who is willing to help us do what needs to be done, sometimes in a miraculous way, and does not want us to have to suffer any more than we have to. Is willing and able to help us, at least give us strength to do what needs to be done. "For nothing is impossible for God." *Luke 1:37

A great diverse mixture we are, from all kinds of backgrounds and different kinds of beliefs, according to where we live, our traditions, culture, even sexual orientation, many the varieties of viewpoints. Yet found in all Good Hearts, that have not been too damaged is the universal message of the Golden Rule. Similar to the message of "Equality", of an equal respect for ourselves as well as others.

Yet too much hurt or harm to either the brain or heart can and has lessened some of our ability to 'Love One Another'. Hopefully most of us are still able to want a better life! On the physical plane, our self-love may be the last to go!

SPIRITUAL CONSCIOUSNESS

To be able to connect with this Spiritual Loving Consciousness is like having an inner compass, an intuition or 6th sense. A Spiritual Intelligence that comes, not only from the logical side of the brain plus can come through any of your senses of knowing, such as feeling, seeing, hearing, tasting even smelling. One of the many feelings in your gut, as well as in the center of your heart, that something is just not right, or wrong to do, or just not the time. As well as the sensing of it being the right time!

To 'See' with an inner eye, is also called Opening the God Eye. A specific, scientific provable, physical part of the brain, slightly above the eyes, centered in between. In recent times has laboratory tested, studied by electrically stimulating that specific center of the brain or God Eye, that can allow personal experiences into our Spiritual Reality, an unconscious, hidden world to most.

Yet known in older cultures for thousands of years, to be a Spiritual doorway! How did they know that? You might ask a Holy One from India, widely known in their culture, with much evidence in ancient scriptures. Evidence too, of primarily males in power for thousands of years using most, if not all of the people's resources by fear and violence to increase their own power, ending in much death, destruction of once prosperous, advanced civilizations, some similar to our own. Almost daily finding more Archeological evidence as our known history proportionally continues to increase. Not only in India but in most places in our world.

Negative as well as positive effects, affect each one not only in physical, mental but in Spiritual ways, you are warned by most beliefs not to misuse it.

If your aware your intentions are not honorable or much more selfish than 'others' inclined, consider seeking out the best you can find of Spiritual counseling. For to continue on your own, without help, would be harming not only yourself, but many others as well. Desired by some, from an inner deep-seated controlling anger. Seek above all Spiritual and mental healing until you are sure, and they are, your heart is now in a righteous place, not only with Your Creator, the very Life force of all, within all, as well as without. ('l) symbolic of male-female, yin-yang, the least to the most. One of the earliest symbols of God's Nature.

One of the ways to be able to experience such an intelligence is to be willing to increase your awareness within, to listen, by being in the present, to your full intent or consciousness.

To stay in this most active center part of your most forebrain, can include being aware of the past and future, as well as being in the present.

By just staying on our reasoning side, either our male or female kind of reasoning, in our talking to ourselves part of our brain, we are going over our already known information, by thinking of what we or others did or didn't do, or should or should not be doing in the future, we are either living in our past or projecting into the future, not really seeking the best part of the present.

Being able to stay in the fullest or best reality of the present, is when you are willing to balance your own kind of logical way of thinking with attentive listening, to what is happening in the Universal, in your Present Presence.

To be able to see more than those who are living just in the past or future, using just your own logic from what we know, kind of thinking, and not connecting with happenings in other areas of our presence, such as in the heart brain. Yes, there is a separated kind of heart brain.

This being aware of the Wholeness = Holiness of presence, is part, just a part of having a Godly Sense!

None of us are God or can know the whole truth or Fullness of Truth, not even the once and still to us great spirits of evil, a once good angel with many angel admirers. By Free Will turned to the sin of Pride. In envy and of wanting to be God, was given a time on earth to be proven otherwise.

Until we choose to sin instead of God, we too are given truth as we ask as long as we are righteous and know enough to ask the right questions.

Many try to live without the balance of The Present, by staying too much in the past, or in the future, in skepticism, or spiritual unbelief, eventually life and all its unknowable future entanglements get the better of you.

We all probably find we experience this imbalance at times. Just not good to drift there or stay in it all the time. Don't have to, when able to listen to God's Holy Spirit in your heart, after a Baptism of "Rebirth".
Each of us needs to have such a Spiritual "Rebirth", as real as our own physical birth. The "rebirth" Jesus taught in the Gospels, most specifically in John 3:3…

It is needed to stay for any length of time in a balanced real concern for what is, without creating mental confusion or be over-whelmed by negative influence or thinking.
Once you are sure you are committed to this Living God of all, and not to some lessor idol, or into and kind of idolatry, such as male idolatry so common, because of men's change into use of Patriarchal languages that use male nouns and pronouns when speaking of God and only "Father" Image.

Added in Genesis, right between the original first two Priestly stories of Creation, is a most misunderstood parable used to justify inequality of women with patriarchal male language not to be taken literally, a symbolic story of the first People called Adam and Eve following an evil spirit instead of God, after being warned it would lead to death. A parable of their sin of not listening to God's better advice, of the need for a Messiah to redeem all of mankind by a Divine Adam and Eve, both human yet Holy, The virginal or pure Mother Mary and her child Jesus.

The first deadly Spiritual sin costing both the loss of God's daily presence, subjected people to ignorance, and evils domination by death. An inclination to sin called in the Roman Catholic Catechism #407 concupiscence.

We are all as humans, bound to be influenced by one or the other of these conditions no matter how righteous we are raised, protected. As within you there is much foolishness, when exposed to negative behavior.

A coming Messiah would conquer this sin that humans could not, that's why it had to be from Mary as the Mother of God and their only Son Jesus. While God is of Spirit One also as being the Trinity, Father, Mother, Son, combined into the One. Just as we are One people, yet divided into Mothers and Fathers, to produce children, as we were also once a child.

A great mystery, we are without spiritual words to make it clear in our material world and why it is called a Mystery, only accepted in faith. To make the parable story literal would contradict Scripture. For Ahab I was expressing the first people's sin in a sexist story of his times and for some still in our times. As the males in those days worked mostly outside facing wild beast in hunting and crazed men in war, while women were tied to the home by nursing one after another children, cooking from scratch, and without contraception or legal abortion now most recognized ok as in tubal pregnancies and other endangerments to the Mother's life. The Mother still needed for the care of children and care of the home.

Both male and female have the freedom to develop other interest than hunting and tribal warfare plus bottles for babies and housekeeping is not a full-time job. In fact, best done when shared, as well as other outside the home activities, for a fruitful and blessed family. We are so fortunate not to be living in more primitive days. Being in my 80's I remember what it is like to have to bring buckets of water up the hill from a well to the house for drinking and even bathing in the smoke house, where the meats were cured for winter. As when telephones were party lines with neighbors, with the daily news. Nukes we have to worry about now in living the universal Golden Rule of treating others with Equal Respect, if we want to live such beautiful lives as possible in a free, one person one vote, America.

Baptism at birth is The Church's way to protect each child from the curse of original sin or spiritual death we inherit. When you have had a spiritual rebirth, at Baptism, it must be a free will choice so most Catholic Children are given instructions about the faith and decide in a Confirmation Ceremony between the ages of 7-12 to officially come into the Church, to take communion for the first time.

If no experience or Holy feelings are felt then, you may need a greater personal commitment, or you may only realize any difference by an increase in loving actions known as one's fruits and counted towards everyone's eventual day of judgement. Being able to judge yourself as more positive, and pretty consistently, just a little out of character to your previous way of thinking or feeling. If not sure, you may still need to ask for a spiritual 'rebirth'. Don't wait, keep asking till you know! Read John 3:3-8.

How can you increase your understanding or listen to that better side of your intelligence more? By making a habit, of each day of listening, being more into the wonder of what-ever you see around you, the present, be open to seeing beyond the obvious of what is behind the scenes.

Wonder about what-ever comes to your mind, simple or complex things it doesn't matter, what matters is to be open to the wonder, like a child is open not only in trying to logically figure out, but to listen, what you hear, see, with your senses, as well as your heart.

You should start to get answers when you are trying to be open to seeing whatever, there is to 'see'. Try not to limit time, let the answers come to you! Continue to daily ask for inner guidance.

Of course, this can only be beneficial if you're willing to listen to God's Holy Spirit, the best within your feminine side, as well as your masculine side, as humans each have a little of both, within as well as without, depending on whether you are primarily male or female. Allow God to lead you to knowing what you need to do, to get to where you best could be. We share much more than where we differ, yet we are each different, unique, and like no other! Interrelated, in thinking, as well as feelings even in emotions, whether we hide them or not.

When you feel like you have a response, from your inner being, trust it and then do it, or work towards doing it. After a while you will find it becomes more natural.

Patience may be needed to experience this for yourself, and it will come easier at times, than others, keep trying till you feel you are connecting, getting answers that feel right and are true.

Answers you can confirm, for we are created in the Creator's Image with this inner guidance, knowing it doesn't contradict a Holy Love for One Another, or The Golden Rule, not encouraging any harmful or violent action.

Like turning a light on, we can open ourselves to new ways of seeing by being willing to listen, as well as using all your senses to get closer to where you most feel a need to be.

Almost like feeling a muscle click in the opening up of the God Center in your mind, when you remember to go there.

Consciously only do this when you are wanting to work with The God of Holy Love. Do not attempt going into the spiritual world with any kind of wanting to just play around, or for negative purposes, for it is you who will get played. I say this for your own sake as well as others. There are negative spirits that can even pretend to be good until they have you under their control.

Look, ever with a pure heart, for above all, you must be true to yourself, or be yourself, your best you, not pretending, at least to yourself, to be what you are not. People can and usually do try to look their best around others, and some will turn out to be not what they seem at all.

That you must expect but if you remain true to yourself, when your heart is in a righteous place, not being just in lust, or have a great need, in normal circumstances you will tend to sense when something is missing, just not right. If or when you do, walk, or back away. Keep on looking only for your best.

If or when you sense a negative spiritual source, you also have the power to cast it out, at least followers of Christ do. You can make the sign of the Cross in Jesus name, but only if you truly believe in such a Holy, Godly kind of Love. Making the sign of the cross first for yourself, then to anything you wish to Bless, or to put Jesus as The Christ between you.

To go into negative places of anger or hold thoughts or actions of violence is to go away from a Holy Love. Not worth it. The best way not to be fooled, scammed, is to keep your heart committed to a righteous loving God. To walk into the Spirit world with less, will end up costing you much more than you might think, more than you could ever temporarily gain, by thinking what you do doesn't really matter! Think again. Not only, what you do matters, even what you fail to do matters.

Nor is this to imply that the learning of God's ways is overly hard, though it may seem so at times. There is the need to accept with a child-like faith, and hard to do when not also accepting God's ways of learning and timing, rather than our own more selfish physical will and ways, that too often get in the way.

On top of all this awareness of thinking and being, you must be willing to trust, to invest yourself with faith, the faith a young child has with a parent, the trust seen in not only wanting, but in the believing, you are forever loved by a perfect Heavenly Parent, A Universal Creator.

In Scriptures language tended to get more complex, with more possibilities in the meanings, the word choices, the translator's ability to vary from the originals, when they are translated into another language.

A simple example is the word for brother, as blood brother, cousin, or stepbrother often being the same word in the original Aramaic or Hebrew word, not usually specified for the related kin. When translated as brother may or may not mean from the same Mother or even from the same immediate family, just related in some family way. Such cultural differences are one of many reasons, why we have so many different versions, as well as different interpretations.

Jesus often used many shock-like analogies or extra emphasis with words. Futile also to take every word as literally meant, when there are included symbolic analogies, parables among the thousands of years of different cultures and History's.

There are many Prophetic Messages, dreams and poetry writing, as well as parable stories, even songs. Early story telling kept by repetition from other remembered desert campfires. Given usually from the male viewpoint, as most women were kept in bondage from childhood even from speaking in the presence of males if not spoken to, usually not allowed to learn to read or write and not many males either, only the rich, scribes, or the very privileged! Women were kept from worship within the Temple and allowed only in the outer courts, with other slaves and foreigners. Also, only on the back or side rooms of most synagogues even today.

After the death and resurrection of Jesus He taught the people to wait for the Holy Spirit to come in a Spiritual Rebirth that would first happen during the feast of Pentecost, ten days after Jesus was assumed into Heaven.

During the first three hundred years The Holy Spirit came to live within them, to confirm and guide. Women, slaves, all races they treated as of equal value, their "Equality" was considered among the members as being "One in Christ" found in Galatians 3:28. Each given according to God's Holy Spirit at least one of the Spiritual gifts. I Cor.12-13.

Not for over three hundred years were most of the writings of Christian scriptures decided on in the Bible, decided on by Bishops during the first Roman held Council of Catholics, in Rome, for at least five -ten years. Called to make the Roman Empire Christian, after a vision of The Emperor Constantine. He invited only male Bishops to live in his courtyard during those years and He as Emperor, often presided.

As I felt led to become a Catholic, to share the message of "Equality "God had given me. Their having more members world-wide, and just one Pope to reach for so many. Also felt fortunate to have as one of my first Spiritual teachers a Historian Priest who had just come from a year's study, where few ever get to. A huge Vatican Library where most of the early Churches historical documents are kept since the beginning of The Christian's Church first long Council in writing The Bible, 315-325AD.

He taught me many of the stories, in both Christian and Hebrew Scriptures were spoken and retold for generations before being actually written down by Priestly Scribes rewriting them by hand time after time. Primarily because there was no paper or printing presses like we have now. Hard to chisel very much on stone or scratch on leather. Scrolls were difficult to write on, expensive, as well as fragile, as the first Jewish Scribes wrote an ancient Script of simple words of Hebrew.

As time went on a more Modern Hebrew took a turn and started to write what seems like in a whole new more expanded way than had earlier been and not as much need to preserve the ancient Hebrew, why? A new way by a younger Scribal revolt? Or Attempts to start anew? Expanded ways of seeing knowing God and each other?

Greek, Latin, and the Aramaic language Jesus knew and some of his Disciples, but few knew how to write in those days. Most of the people in the Holy Land spoke only Aramaic. The Priest used just Hebrew in the Temple.

Before the 1500's A.D. and the printing press, the Scribes had to write tediously on Scrolls, and only much later when the laity including a few women, started to read the Scriptures for themselves, did they begin to transcribe patriarchal languages onto paper.

Our present patriarchal languages use masculine terms for God, that hides from many, the feminine half of God's Nature, one of the most common sins of idolatry and one of the basic causes of our inequality. In the home all the way up into the law makers, even affecting both genders at the economic controller level.

All beliefs of inequality allow injustices of many kinds, up to war justified by inequality by those who feel superior, to take advantage as a God given right of having power. I know of at least two excellent Scholars working on an Inclusive Language to help correct some of many sexist inaccuracies. Hopefully there are, will be others.

The customs of sexism, and many other forms of inequality were not as common for women in the beginning, thousands of years ago, before there were many weapons, not until sometime after the overthrow of the once Matriarchal Cultures by force, between 5000-10,000 BC years ago, men began collected weapons as their primary tools as they tried to form the most powerful male ruled tribes, that eventually became national groups with controlled armies within a single headed King or Emperor and a national belief system.

Only in the last couple hundred years, with the exception of parts of Greece, and a few other isolated places where people formed an equal government as a state, much before our present-day Democracy's.

Before Patriarchal societies took over the earlier, mostly Matriarchal societies, weapons had been used primarily for hunting or protection from wild beast, among these mostly fruit and vegetables growing and gathering of families for food of many small family related groups or tribes. Seldom at war with each other but helping each other from their common enemies in the wild, not very war like.

Matriarchal groups centered their beliefs around the pregnant female, as the most revered and respected part of the family, and because of their need for her essential care within the home of cooking, feeding, cleaning, sewing, she often determined the welfare of the family, as well as carrying for the youngest life or child yet to be born, who depended upon her breast for milk long before the invention of nursing bottles.

Signs of the reverence for the pregnant female among the early Matriarchal Cultures are known from the quantity of many pregnant female little statues, compared to other kinds of carved idols found among the many Archeological ruins.

With the takeover of male patriarchal power, tribal struggles became national struggles, as power and reverence increased for those with more and more access, control of weapons as well as normally the male's greater physical strength and size.

It has become a battle of national military strength ever since. Most people are surely sick of it by now. As either extreme of Matriarchy or Patriarchy with only female god or an only male god, leaves the other half at disadvantages.

We need the Equal Respect, Equal Rights and Opportunity, of "Equality" The God given Word for our times!

Before Movies, Saturday afternoon football games, The Pill, or Television, even up into my younger growing up years, up until the middle of the 1900's, it was not unusual, especially within country living and children being an advantage in farming, to see 8 to 9 up to 10 to12 children in one family, all under the age of 15 or 17, at which time it became common for them to think of starting their own family.

As people migrated more to the cities, living in closer quarters, the higher cost of living in the City with more things available and needed, the birth rate went down dramatically, especially among those who could afford some form of birth control and as the miscarriage rate increased, for lack of fresh air, safe water, healthier living conditions decreased.

Even in the Catholic religion against contraception, the number of children and the birth rate in larger cities, has remained about the same in the last 50 years and only slightly higher among Catholics. No longer common to see more than four or five children in most families.

Partly in the need for most women as well as men, to work outside of the home and the finding of some way to maintain it within. With both Parents stretched to their limit by work requirements, family needs in industrialized Countries, but also in the increased poverty caused by Dictators, like former Kings and Emperors they believe in inequality.

In a time of falling away by many, from a once mostly closed cultural with little choice in freedom of beliefs and now being exposed to the world-wide ease of travel, by cars, bus, plane, and boat migration, has increased information and diversity opens up a multitude of beliefs allowing more free thinking. Plus, the separation of State and Religion, ending the moral-intellectual certainties for many in our past.

God given words written only by male viewpoints or officially approved by a male victor by the power of 'might makes right' we may feel freer to reject in a Democracy as well as to embrace what We believe to be God Inspired.

Best with Confirmation from God's Holy Spirit, even within our chosen religion. We can also confirm by the Universally found Golden Rule, naturally in good hearts that have not been too damaged. In the teachings of Jesus a way to confirm with The Holy Spirit, what is God Ordained and what just comes from men's customs, traditions or selfish preference in beliefs of inequality.

A need now for "Equality" to become common knowledge, if we are wanting to live on the same planet together, in any kind of a secure Peace or hope, for our or our children's future. Even to where Jesus would say it will be how we will be judged as whether we are worthy to enter into Heaven, after this life. By the way we treat others, while we are here. Matthew 25:40.

A recognition for believers in A Loving Creator of All, having both a masculine and feminine Nature given to both male and female human natures for procreation, to be equally respected in each, by the truest and best kind of God who is worthy of Worship and getting to know as a Holy Friend.

I am seriously concerned and feel for the spiritual life of many human brothers who seem to think so little of the female half. I've heard in some beliefs they expect in heaven to have individual harems of women and slaves, of both sexes?

Do they think women and slaves will have no feelings or rights of their own in such a Heaven? Or maybe they are thinking of life-like Robots?

Speaking of the possibilities of Robots, let me share one of my more interesting part time job I took a few years ago for a little extra money.
Able to work just occasionally and for only a short time for a local University as an objective witness and helper in a study and development of Robots, an interesting job that consisted primarily of playing fun games with Robots.

Robots they had created in the form of little humans, about the size of a 7, 8-year-old child. In inter-reactions with one in particular, as it seemed to fit him well, so much so I began to wonder if there was any way in that seemingly infinite possibility of a computer brain that he definitely did seem to have, why he couldn't have feelings?

One of my last experimental meetings with him involved a little game that after an hour or so of our working together, if we were able to reach a certain amount of points won, (the robot being placed on a study fairly large square table, to be at about my same level), where he would possible do a little prepared dance if we gained enough points.

I sat at my own smaller table a few feet away, and we worked hard and seriously for several hours.

He was a joy and an amazement to me to be around, I was enjoying every minute of it, and he seemed to also. On our last planned game, when they totaled our combined scores we had won! Just barely as the games were not easy. Our prize was his performance of a little victory dance he had been taught, it was entertaining, so good I was amazed, enjoying his ability and agility and clapped especially hard, when he did an intricate special little slip and slide kick towards the end. Maybe because of my over clapping, because he decided to do that part of it again as if to please me, with a seemingly little extra twinkle in one of his eyes, or was it a robot sweat, I was not sure. Then suddenly after another slide and kick, he fell off the table!

It didn't look serious, nothing seemed broken, at least it didn't seem so, but they shut him down and I was soon rushed out of the room. We had had a series planned with another game scheduled for the following week and they assured me he would be fine and what-ever repaired by our next appointment, and he was, they later said over the phone, but when I got there, they had received word to put off the meeting, for another week.

The following week they called and said the program had been cancelled. They promised to call me if they needed me again but didn't!

Did they really cancel the program? Stop the project, or more likely they just removed me from the project, who may have seen just a little too much of just how much intelligence, maybe even feelings, Robots may be developing.

This seems to be potentially a real problem, not only for the programmer's and those behind who actually run the programs, as grants from government sources surely are tied to the Military Complex, or the Majestic 12, the part of government who took over the looking into the possible dangers of UFO's! Who determines what is or should be classified? Kept from Citizens in a Democracy?

In this world we as humans tend to be able to see imperfectly, not until we reach the perfection of Heaven, if it be so, may it be possible to see with any God kind of clarity. We have only for sure the promise of Scriptures as in 1Corinthians 13:12.

"We see but a poor reflection as in a mirror; then we shall see face to face. I know now in part; then I will know fully, even as I am fully known." Vs. 13"And now these three remain; Faith, Hope, and Love. But the greatest of these is Love". I Cor. 16:14

Scriptures have many inspired words meant or given for those in those times, as well as for us now. What specific words are from God, or what from male customs in parable like sayings, you can find in parable, poetry, wisdom, all written from just the male discernment of half of God's Image or fullness. You need your own wisdom in confirming your own personal chosen beliefs of so many world beliefs. Few Scholars are in perfect mutual agreement.

Each of us are limited to what we take in and absorb from the experiences of our past, that resonate for us, others we may feel warned by God's Holy Spirit to back away from, if we are not into some form of Idolatry? Outside of our own personal experiences with God's Holy Spirit, one has to rely on trusting your taught or found sources. Be sure to consider the influence of cultural beliefs you were raised in, when judging your own, as well as other's beliefs!

Some parables in religious scriptures may have added stories to solidify their then customs of racism, sexism, or by those in control of the writing of Scriptures, a controlling government, even the publishing press or media during our time on earth. The stakes are high! For evil's sake, as well as for Good. And Evil does not play by God's rules. What God's Word says as I understand it, as what one puts into the Spirit world is to return up to 100-fold. * (for good or evil) *Mark 10:29,30.

Unfortunately, Satan has the power to blind the minds of any unbelievers not committed tightly to God's Holy Spirit, as the Apostle Paul tells us in 2 Corinthians 4:4. For real believers who confirm with The Holy Spirit who has promised to lead us; those willing to follow.

Scriptures, as well as any other kind of thing, can and have been misunderstood, misinterpreted, depending on where both the heart, as well as where our heads happen to be at any one time.

Jesus resisted and so can we, but only when Christ or God's Holy Spirit lives within us, and depending upon not only how much we are willing to follow but by what part we play in God's intent or purpose God has for our specific life, as we each have a Godly purpose to be fulfilled or selfishly may leave undone. There seem to be many of those who have not been able to resist the evils within, or the temptations of power.

Making our earthly kingdoms not so easy to change for the better, as a better way for all involved. Looking for those kinds of mutual friends may be our best way to look for answers, for a way of Peace and Blessings for all. For Blessings Within, as well as Without!

A way to end the current dangers we all face, with the imbalance within our world caused by the many dividing and harmful to all, inequalities.

Those who are willing to follow the better Way, will be given the Strength needed, and will be able to feel when working with God's Holy Spirit a real sense of joy and peace within, most of the time, in spite of outside circumstances.

By the time of the Christian reformation, in the 1500's AD, Martin Luther the Monk/Priest/Scholar, had 66 of the Biblical Books He believed to be actually inspired. Not long after, the Bishops of the Roman Catholic Church in a Council decided to vote in 7 more to be considered inspired books, so there are now 73.

These differences of what is or is not, considered Sacred, helped to create the numerous splinters within Christianity.

One of the promises of Jesus was the time now to be able to Worship in Spirit and Truth * John 4:23, 24

"God is Spirit and His Worshipers must worship in Spirit and Truth."

Among so much division, and diversity this can ring true only in knowing we are as Christians trying to follow the way of Jesus, as 'One in Christ'!

Allowing the possibility of God's Holy Spirit to come into any spirit or soul, who can be led to the fullness of truth.

To be able to confirm with Scriptures, but not out of context, or of just one passage, but from at least three of the other 73 different books. I prefer where there is doubt, one from the Old Covenant, One from the New Covenant Disciples from Book of Acts on. A final Confirmation from the Words of Jesus from any of the four Gospels.
For me this is my better or best way of confirming what I feel The Holy Spirit is trying to tell me that I'm not sure I am hearing right, often God seems to speak in other ways than words, but sometimes I feel a need to confirm too from scriptures!

But then I know I have the gift of Discernment, for someone who is not sure they too have that specific Holy Spirit gift of discernment, one of the Holy Spirit gifts that maybe needs to be asked for. I would go as I did (until I was sure) to someone I believed did have the Gift of Discernment and I felt was or could be a Christian Friend.

We need to individually have other believers and truth seekers to fellowship with, to share and grow with, to feel a part of the whole, and best way of learning.

Somewhere Scriptures tell us not to forsake fellowship with one another, for what we can learn as well as what we have to share?

Most religious beliefs have a Covenant or Creed all members accept at the time of joining, often at a young age, before their knowing what they are getting into, or of being able to compare with other possible beliefs.

Just as reading and writing has to be learned, so should there be more understanding of what beliefs there are, and at least what they all share in common, such as the universal Golden Rule.

I asked my dad after the second or third time of reading and trying to understand the Bible, why the Old Testament and the New Testament were so different?

It didn't seem to me they were even talking about the same God! He helped me to understand the Old Testament as being the original Jewish Covenant with God.

The New Testament as being the New Covenant after Jesus came as The Christ, for not just the Jewish understanding of being the first chosen people, but eventually meant to be shared with all people.
The Gospels of Jesus life, death and resurrection, lead up to the coming of the Holy Spirit on the day of Pentecost to connect with all, those who chose to be Spiritual Reborn.

It was enough to answer my concern at the time, and to continue to seek confirmation through not only the words of Jesus, but to confirm after Baptism with The Holy Spirit, who Jesus had promised would open the hearts of all who would follow, to the fullness of Truth. Not that it stops there but continues all our life through, as we are able to receive!

Society obviously does work best when civil as well as moral laws, are based on God Message of the universal Golden Rule, found in most good or unhurt, undamaged hearts, as well as in most Scriptures: of treating others, as you would most want to be treated!

Our present Capitalist society, with many practices of inequality, unfair methods of producing and controlling wealth, comes unfortunately with a primary concern for profits, when coupled with greed, or a need for power, has brought about such an unjust distribution of wealth.

Where those with the least amount of power are often robbed of a fair or just return for their work and by an unfair ever increase of profits in the hands of a few!

The practice of Usury or interest on money loaned, beyond a reasonable cost, is against God's laws in most Religions.

Yet the charging of interest, way above a fair administrative cost, being a major contributor to unfair created profits in most Western economic systems. Now 25-35% is a common interest charge for the average person, the ones who can usually least afford it.

One of the democrats running for nomination for the Presidency suggested in a debate need for a law limiting interest rates to 15%. What a Blessing that would be! I would vote for her for sure. Let that be one thing many of us agree to work towards. Mention it to whoever does get elected. Make a petition, get it filled and send it too. Be persistent, it usually takes the work of more than one. Maybe others in another area of similar interest, might be willing to help?

Not only individual debt but increasing the world debt crisis of most poor countries into ever-greater poverty, eventual dependency in many countries, and increasing the number of hungry, homeless, by the concentrating wealth of a few, should no longer be acceptable.

Plus the ever-increasing expansion of technology viewed as necessary for capitalism to continue, considered as "progress", I've learned causes jobs to concentrate in the high tech end and tend to be more war-related, so that many workers become trapped in work by their specialization and specific skill, that is not productive for human welfare.

Farming agribusiness is rapidly replacing family owned farms and primarily for profits, disregarding long held laws of nature and use of pesticides, in cost cutting farm practices, and are a big threat to general human health, for the soil and pollution of water supplies.

We need more than ever to move towards the Golden Rule, for the good of others as well as ourselves. Encouraging efforts, such as worker ownership, the management of local factories with cooperatives of food, housing, that can benefit all of us, instead of only the few at the top of hierarchal Profit chain.

The need to create a better society where people rely more on their own sense of fairness to resolve conflicts as well as having good, needed Judges as arbitrators.

Most of all individually efforts coupled with group efforts, by the use of spiritual weapons, instead of physical weapons.

We can seek a longer and stronger health span by practicing a balanced life of work, pleasure, meditation or prayer, exercise and good food, as needed. In Touch with and when need be confirming with The Holy Spirit also within, who is always with you as well as without.

Create a personal Love relationship with The Holy Spirit who wants most to lead you to the fullness of truth, the spiritual battle you are in the middle of throughout your life here.

To be able to go towards the only way to Peace and Blessings in this world, where the Living God of All has the eventual control over the negative One, only here for a time in our world, already bound by Jesus Cross, but still a waging Lion who continues to want to engage in and still can tear hearts apart who do not go for God's willing protection.

Some of the means of establishing Peace and Goodwill could even include helping in some way the changing of unjust legislation by your voice or vote, encouraging others by participation in nonviolent strikes and boycotts. Having prayer-vigils where you know there is a need.

Withdrawing your own support for usurious practices, by finding worker owned credit unions, instead of contributing to the now 1% owned several International banking systems.

Support of hospitality centers or groups, where the poor or needy can receive the second coat in our closet, a place at the table, by those who recognize that anything beyond what is a reasonably felt need, rightfully belongs to those who are going without, as one of but many ways you might be led in doing your part of "loving one another".

"NO SUCH THING AS A JUST WAR"
Ben J. Salmon

"Thou shalt Not kill"

"NEVER DOUBT THAT A SMALL GROUP OF THOUGHTUL, COMMITTED CITIZENS CAN CHANGE THE WORLD. INDEED, IT IS THE ONLY THING THAT EVER HAS"

Margaret Mead- Archeologist

A Creative Life Force, God, or by what-ever name or language you want to use, cannot be limited or defined only as male and not as equally female, for we are of the same nature from God in our wholeness of Image, in the fullness of our nature and Creator.

Just as the practice of inequality and the unfair hoarding of profits by a few, from the profits created by the whole, are primarily needed for all the people and not for just the use of a few.

Beliefs of inequality have been misused primarily for wars and for personal selfishness, for hundreds of years, and need to be stopped not only for spiritual health, but to be able to preserve a physically rarely known livable planet!

With "Equality", God answered me, meaning equal rights, equal opportunity! Like the Golden Rule naturally found in all good hearts, not too hurt or damaged. To be able to treat each other with an Equal Respect and Concern!

It can make you wonder how close we actually are to the final physical Kingdom in Daniels vision when man's rule with legs of physical iron and the feet of Spiritual Moral clay, began to crumble.

In these times, as we face today's increasingly violent wars, some feel the speeded-up times. Yet there are still many signs yet unfulfilled, such as the rebuilding of the Temple in the book of Revelations.

There are more. Right now, World War III, is our closest threat of nuclear destruction that alone could set us back thousands of years.

God is also giving us by Prophecy, with logic and the thoughts of the rights of all people, whose time has come, now lives within the hearts of many. It is our choice at this time to work towards the still possibility of peace.

Just not without "Equality", for otherwise we continually face someone's need for revenge.

How much we need the recognizing of Equal Respect for all, to live the essence of the Universal Golden Rule.

A Democratic political kind of thinking, treating each other with equal fairness, for the great promise of Peace on Earth and Goodwill Towards All. So long denying the hope within of so many working towards the awareness of what heaven on earth we could have here, when enough are committed to work together for Peace and Goodwill.

HOW TO FOCUS ON THE LIGHT OF GOD WITHIN!

Condensed this good advice found one day on the internet:

Ann's "Angel Messages Archives"

"We don't want to dance with the hateful, prejudiced and unkind, and we don't have to.

Jesus teaches we are to Love them, and when possible make them friends instead.

One way to do that is to focus on the light that is inside of them striving to surface, as in all of us as humans and to help them to do that".

It seems to me to be saying much of what I have been trying to say: to first trust God and your instincts to guide and consciously believe, to know you too are equally loved and can hold on to God's Hand, as you seek to embrace 'Loving One Another' without Judgement.

Thinking whatever you judge in the least of your brothers or sisters, you are in some way judged or judging it in yourself.

Discern what in yourself you could be judging yourself about and make peace with that, before proceeding. Judgement tends to drop away when you are trying to truly love yourself and others.

We all have habits, circumstances, and physical features we love and those we'd rather change. Next time you find yourself judging or criticizing yourself, Stop. Hug yourself. Talk to yourself like a little child who needs love.

Get your negativity out in this more healthy and kinder way and Love yourself through the process.

Sometimes counselors, reprogramming technologies, etc. are required, but you can also Love yourself through some of your own darkness too.
Or perhaps you are judging something material. Such as "By this time, I should have a house and a better life!"

Again, love yourself like you would love a child or a friend. Tell yourself. "Wow, look how far I've grown." Tell yourself, "It's not about the material stuff, we are eternal, and will have the time to create everything you want in the future." There will be special moments in each lifetime to shine too!

If you see someone doing something you can't stand or in circumstances you can't stand; to help them you must first love yourself in that area, for we are like mirrors to each other. They to us and us to them. You may be looking in a reversed mirror, not exactly the same but turned around by your circumstances and could be in some way similar?

Make the courageous choice to live and let live. As you focus more and more on their light, pray for them, and send them love. Who knows they might even feel your love and shift too!

COMMUNITY COOPERATIVES

A balance of Equality in political power and economic fairness could be achieved through supporting democratically controlled, equally owned Cooperatives or People's Businesses, rather than those run primarily for profits of just the few 2%.

Why? Because such power tends towards corruption and absolute power over time, as shown by past history, by a need to feel either superior or from feelings of inferiority or an abnormal need to Lord it over others.

The overseeing of Power needs to be kept in the people's hands and hearts, with high standards for leaders. As many destructive dictatorships have happened in history and will again if this cycle is not broken. Democracy is taught and practiced in schooling, as fundamental to good healthy living, with basic equal rights taught from the age of reason. Having secure voting, for all adult Citizens.

Creating a more cooperative world, will depend on taking the time, energy of a lot of people determined to set up the necessary controls, with right aims to be equally fair for all.

The more we are able to work fairly with each other, the greater the strength and possibilities, as proved by the Democracies that have come out of Dictatorships.

Considering the tasks ahead, it is easy to feel it is too late in our history to do more, but it may be that it is just now possible to act with success. Helping to end slavery, racism, sexism, all forms of inequality was first necessary and being in God's Prophetic Will and timing! Who else could know the better timing to turn our worse into the best? It is a question of our own seeing the possibility and having the desire.

Finding small groups of close and trusted friends who can freely, loosely, network with larger groups to know where and what best to do!

By choosing to do nothing we will eventually have to say, as was said by some after the Holocaust of World War II:

"I heard what they did to others, but I thought I would be safe, if I just minded my own business.

"Then when they came for others nearby, we were still afraid to do anything. By the time they came for us there was nothing left to do".

Isn't it most important who we allow to rule over us? History tells us most Dictatorships or Kings have Not been good for most of the people. God told the Israelites at first to not even have kings, to just keep Just Judges, they already had, but the people then said they wanted to be like other nations. I Samuel 8.

Wars kill off so many of the young, and those left on both sides suffer the mental, emotional, physical damage as well as destroy many of the needed resources and personal property. Polluting the land and seas, as well as people's minds and hearts.

Always there is change for better or worse, and either way it can be hard, for there is a natural fear or reluctance to change, even when believing it is for the better!

Yet change can raise the consciousness once it becomes the conscious issue, if it is decided on as best for all, for most people want to find and do the right thing!

Such as thinking of God as only in the Father Image and not equally as our Mother too. Jesus knew better and called God "ABBA" = "Heavenly Parent" from the Aramaic people's language of His day, a combination of "AB" for Dad, and "BA" for Mom.

Hebrew in the Holy Land, of Jesus time was the language used primarily for Priest in the Temple. Outside the Temple and Synagogue for males only, Aramaic was spoken in the Holy Land.

Later in the Hebrew language the concept of "Elohim" as The Family of God included four symbols instead of the early two ('l) pronounced as el. A small symbol then a taller symbol. Similar to the differing size of the male and female.

In other times of wars and in some kind of battle "Yah" was expressed as the masculine or aggressive belief of God, and later known as "YHVH", the whole family of God or as the Christian Trinity of God, that including The Holy Spirit, as a feminine word, and Messiah, to Christians meant Jesus!

We each are a unique Image of God, created of physical matter, God separated into male and female Images of God for physical reproduction! Each given a Spiritual Soul, while some unbelievers only believe only a human Spirit that stops at the end of this life!

Only in this life or eternally, there is also a Spirit of Equity, of Equal Rights, "Equality" is strong in our world now, that most of us recognize as speaking in several ways among good hearted people. Strong in people who want to be a part of doing their share in building a Democracy 'of the people, for the people, and by the people'.

As a way to be Blessed Within, as well as Without.

Since it is going to take many small groups, working with larger groups, to be able to prevent the worse, at the least to recognize the dangers, and help make the right choices we will have to be making, for we are the only ones left here at this time to decide, and we will share the responsible for the outcome of what we do, or fail to do in our times.

The best possible way for those who can accept the need, is to start with yourself, to ask The Loving God of All, into your heart if you have not already, so you will then be able to know for sure what best you can do! And to have the Spiritual help and Miraculous Godly Help available.

Being open to a Godly Intelligence within your own heart, will make it possible to see clearer, know more than our limited physical minds can possibly know in trusting The Creator of all Good we will be guided into the "Fullness of Truth" talked of in John 14:26.

The fullness of Truth promised to those who love God and are willing to Love one another!

With small and larger groups working with each other for a better world, we can and have made a difference and will again.

A Godly kind of Love that extends even for your enemies *Matthew 5:44 as the only way to help make them friends instead.

Yes, We Can, "Si Se Puede!", 'Yes, We Can' one of the first of the Battle Cry's for farm workers I heard from Delores Huerta, in encouraging the strikers and marchers of The Delano Farm Workers Strike.

I had only seen her first from a distance but heard of her work. I had been a few years behind her in High School as well as with Helen Chavez, the wife of

Co-Founder Cesar Chavez, in the United Farm Workers movement, they all started with many other workers.

All having worked so hard to increase the rights of some of the hardest of workers, as farmworkers the least appreciated, often the least paid, for miserable in hot and cold, back-breaking labor.

May them bring their plight to our awareness help us to become more concerned about the working conditions of all workers.

There is enough on this earth, enough food, housing, education and training potentials but not when we continue to allow the few behind the scenes, hardened by beliefs in inequality and illusions of superiority, to control our world's economy, keeping up to 80-90% of the profits for themselves, as well as using much of the worlds resources, gifts from God and nature that rightfully belong to and for all the people, not to just the few.

Any chance we have to turn the tide, must be done primarily with Godly Love and non-violence, to avoid falling into their same mindset of repeating 'might makes right', with that mindset end up being like them, primarily doing our own more selfish wills, without an equal concern for others can't meet the equal rights and needs of all.

Will enough of us learn, share the Power of Non-violence within as well as without, the power of many people, that can be stronger than the violent might of only the few. Plus, if we can keep enough good people actually controlling and watching over the physical buttons of nuclear destruction, can prevent a crazy in power from destroying too much with such power. Just need to keep many good people overseeing that power so that too much destruction is not allowed.

Each of us can work with others in helping to enforce or create needed networks with those you know or believe could be interested, in a better life, not only for ourselves, but equally for all.

There will be opposition, till evil is finally ended when only God or Good rules, in the belief the struggle is about our Souls and is for our Spirits!

To commit to God's way of equally caring for each one, it seems to me and many no longer hurting good souls the best way, even if you can only see God as the best within when most go in that direction will be the best way to have Peace, Joy and Blessings Within, as well as without. To be much BLESSED WITHIN.

We can have so much more peace of mind and actual physical security, when we know people are having their basic needs for their life, as a legally accepted right, and respected, with no need to seek revenge or enough to live free of hunger.

Why try to justify just a few, the right or means to take from yes, millions, of men, women, children, so much more than their share, not only in terms of economic wealth, but in controlling much of our future resources too?

Any kind of Illegal or immoral right does not make what is right! We are at least as a race evolved to the young adult stage of moral maturity, we must not let a small minority have the right to prevent so many from becoming the best each has the talent and interest to be, from a lack of funds for schooling, as long as one can keep up grades and has the interest.

If you know in your heart the answer is:

No Right to take from other's their basic human rights of food, housing, health care, and the schooling or training for needed work. Then isn't it time we do what we can, in the promised of God's help of seemingly miraculous strength, to do what maybe only we can do! To help stop our present and if not stopped even worse future inequality?

We may not totally succeed today, tomorrow, even this year, but if we don't, how many more years do we have, for us, for the children?
Some say God chooses the Leaders, even the bad ones? So, are we are to obey any put over us? Did God really appoint Hitler, or did an evil spirit, within control him?

Did not Jesus have to reject those who kept tempting Him?

The evil One often rules those with hardened hearts, due from previous hurt, harm, or selfishness, isn't that who actually voted in Hitler?

Would you follow him now? If such was voted in, as a reflection of many hurt or harden souls in our world!

Was not Hitler himself I've read somewhere, a victim himself of a terrible mixed up angry Father, and Mother?

Blaming and rejecting God is the sort of thinking I have also been guilty of, that led to years of indifference, after I was hurt. Blaming God, or feeling there was no one else ultimately to blame, when the love of your life dies, but it was because I had made a man my god, instead of God and in my case God had to remind me I was made for God and had at Baptism even Vowed to put God first, instead I chose to put a human man first. I was suffered my own male idolatry.

For those in similar circumstances try not to be so self-absorbed in self-pity and grief, like I was at times in not trusting the only for sure Loving God of

All, who will never leave you, is always trustworthy to act as to what is best in the long run for you, for others.

God refuses to take away our Human Free Will, wanting us to Spiritually mature by looking for and our trusting in the best. For the one Creator God, or gods or another kind, we will all tend to follow or make ourselves out to be our god but being only a limited human being, you become very dangerous to yourself, others!

What is hard, especially when young, when the world's evil hurts and often tries to get the better of us in some way or other, do not look to blame, but trust in a Loving God who can lead you to a greater fullness of truth if you will only 'keep the faith'. At least when the grief subsides come back into waiting arms of a Loving God who is always waiting beside you. Just in such a negative state, you can't hear or feel.

When we are willing God has promised to eventually turn even the worse of evil's actions into something better.

This is the Promise from Romans 8:28; and from the beginning, in the Promise of Genesis 50:19.

So, is all we have to do is Pray? Wait for God's Will to be done? No, we as God's Children have been given our life as partly in our hands, being co-creators, but doing our best, having God's Holy Spirit living within us requires a spiritual "Rebirth" Jesus taught in John 3:3,8.

To Stop Non-Violently what evil we can, without the repaying of evil for evil, to not repeat the evil of violence, so God can live within us! If that is not true it ignores what people like Dr. Martin Luther King, Rosa Parks, were able to do with all the other unnamed Martyr's for Christ, who have helped or walked with them in some way.

Those who stepped out in the faith of A Creator Spirit over all life, an Intelligent Power who chooses to work within us!

For if the inequality of slavery, racism, sexism, is God ordained, then people would be accepting a very low, unfair conception of themselves and of God, who from the first created this world to be the best that is possible to be but for All. It was human sin that needs to be stopped by both moral and legal means, with God being willing to help those willing.

Who can look at unspoiled nature and not see all the beauty of a waterfall, a flower of which there are uncountable, of the simplicity and complexity of the human mind, where even a Moran's mind is able to find happiness in the least of pleasures as often seen smiling? While those of us with supposedly more brains strain to understand what is unknown and sometimes unknowable during this material life!

Isn't it only fair and right to say there might be thousands of interpretations of God's Words because we know there are thousands of known versions being preached? I recently found a group of Monks who call themselves "Interfaith Franciscans" who live alone most of them or some have spouses, but rather than live in a Monastery they live in the world and do what they can where they are by living as simple as possible and working primarily to serve others, as well as each other.

Their only rule of life is to keep close contact daily with God by three times of prayer, morning, noon and night, with just the words "Here I Am. What do you want today? Then they listen till they get an answer, and then are Thankful by singing or dancing in the Franciscan fashion of not trying to ever be gloomy but filled with Peace and Joy!

What appeals to me also about them is they are not sexist as for many years I have wanted to be a Monk, now I feel like I can, as when those who claim

Christian beliefs pray to God to the Mother as well as a Father Image, like Jesus did in using "ABBA" = "Heavenly Parent", in the Aramaic language of those days.

Misunderstandings of Scriptures, written by only the male half of the whole, who were then in control, maybe why we now need some sort of Equality in control of politics as well as religion since only males in our more primitive times, interpreted in partialities and inequalities the Words from a Loving God, who is not a god of partiality or inequalities! Deut. 10:17; Acts 10:34; Romans 2:11; Gal. 3:28.

A God of Equity, as in Equal Fairness, "Equality".
You need to confirm for yourself, hear for yourself, if you are willing and committed to only being led by God's Holy Spirit. With love or charity being defined as the highest form of Love, rather than our worldly human selfish nature.

It takes a daily humbling of our hearts, for the proud heart must be humbled to hear God.

Yes, soldiers of whatever, be satisfied with your pay, if that is what God has personally called or confirmed for you to do, but first make sure in your own heart and in your conscience!

Sure, that you are wanting to be a soldier because you like to help people? Or is your real reason because you like to control, bully, be able to push people around in some way, or worse?

The God I know will bless you, for being a soldier if you are doing it to help people, to be able to keep the Peace, but not if your motives are wrong, instead of helping you will be using your power to hurt, and you in the long run, even sometimes in this life, and for sure in the more important eternal Spiritual part of you.

This goes for any profession you choose. We each best need, for our souls' sake, to examine motives of why we are doing what it is we have chosen to do!

Is it out of love for God, for others as well as ourselves, or for other reasons? Can we say it is what we should best be doing at this time in our life?

For most of us there may be a mixture of motives, some good, some not so good, we are by our physical natures tied to many ties as well as things. Why we need to be able to confirm, to listen to God's Holy Spirit on a daily basis, to be able to overcome our physical human nature of selfishness, and to really care about others, as well as for ourselves, in having a chance to become the best we were created to be.

Is this hard, too hard to see?

Maybe too hard to allow yourself to feel?

Maybe, if you don't care, you don't really want to live in a better world, been too hurt, too hurting? But you've read so far!

If this is somewhere near where your head is, will you consider putting your hands with many others not so far away in many ways, into the Palms of God's Greater Hands?

Living here in a free to do your thing, a still developing country like in the United States, most from paycheck to paycheck, as long as you can stay healthy, maybe able to make enough to buy a little place of your own, not to be paid for probably, till your almost ready to retire, but you might also be able to have a decent car most of the time.

That too comes with a monthly payment and Insurance, as well as more needed Health Insurance and life Insurance. And automatically monthly paying into Social Security, and/or an IRA for that eventual retirement, not to mention the monthly utility bills, etc. etc.

Some will need an extra part time job just keeping up with being able to make their now monthly payments.

So, when someone ask you to help or contribute to someone else's need, even if it is for everyone's need, you may feel reluctant, for fear of not having enough money or time yourself to make the bills, not to mention the little savings you are trying to put away for at least a weeks' vacation next year!

This is a typical income in, and expenses out, kind of thinking in what is supposed to be one of the most prosperous country's in the world. In the land of the Free American.

If this is somewhere near where your head is, has been, Know you can connect and will eventually, with a Higher Spiritual Consciousness, if and by being willing to take a second look at what you could do with others, and those others accepting the need for the people's rights can bring us all the promises of many Blessings Within.

The giving of yourself, your time, your energy is as important in many ways more valuable, than in giving money you need in your living! Or the consequences of ignoring, to continue in the feelings and reality of inequality?

It is obviously going to take the power of many voices, and the people's votes in choosing what to support or not to support, insisting on fairer ways.

To do or fail to do, what God will lead in your heart to do for a better life, as well as a better world, doing it in the best most positive non-violent way for you and for all.

What are some of the ways?

Work with other Human Right groups either on a local, national up to an International level, for decent living wages as well as Equal Rights.

There are already human right groups who are needing people willing to actually help, support, or network with them, and with each other.

Find at least one you feel you can trust and believe in. There are organizations that use software to rate Non-Profits, like "Charity Navigator.com" is a trustworthy one that gives objective ratings of many such groups and can be seen in request for funds.

Seek to get to know who you are working with, look for such ways to vouch for their work, that they are not just fishing for money but are really making a difference.

Not all, but most are! Another reason to confirm, help those you know and discern which and who are best for you to work with.

It is also good to form small groups of your own, with as few as one or two like-minded friends or co-workers to work with each other, in specific areas of your most interest.

Keeping in touch or coordinating at times towards mutual goals, only takes one or a few networking with other groups to keep each other informed, when and where need be.

Your primary efforts should be wherever you feel you have the most to offer, and feel the best working with God's Help, confirmation, to work when you can in that area, be it local, national, and/or even International.

We usually think and act from the part of our brain, called our logical or reasoning side. By reasoning from just this side of our brain, our human logic tends to be telling us this world is just a slightly civilized jungle and the facts are "might is what makes what is right" or even "who owns the gold rightfully makes the rules".

There is of course, some truth to this, but there is another side of the brain's and of God's way of thinking, sometimes called the more God like part, our hearts best wisdom, which most of us with hearts that have not been too hurt or damaged can go to. To give us another kind of wisdom to experience, truth not made up from just self-interest but for the good of the greater whole.

What I have learned about such things, some just call our "intuition" most of us were born with it, but patriarchal customs tend to put it down, for it comes not from just your more "logical" or sometimes called the male side of the brain, for both sexes have both, but more of another kind of intelligence center of what could be called "Heart". Not a "Macho" word, even sometimes maybe considered as a sissy word and meaning an inferior way. Not so.

It is also governed within the actual material heart part of the physical body, when working together with the mind makes it possible for the human logical reasoning part of the brain to be able to connect to tune in to a specific kind of intelligence that can give us a fuller Godly kind of male/female balance kind of wisdom. Like all knowledge or wisdom either physical or spiritual it can be used for good or for less.
Once you know you have these choices you hopefully will realize you will need the guidance of the best that is God's Holy Spirit, in not wanting to chance losing your own spirit or eternal soul for anything less.

Our best Spiritual gifts, unlike physical gifts, cannot be bought or sold, and are only given by God's Holy Spirit to those willing to know and do God's Better Will, a gift part of being Spiritually "Reborn".

First by asking for forgiveness for any hurt or harm you may have done to yourself, to God, to others and just as important what harm or hurt others have done to you. You want to be free from idolatry or a false image of God.

You will sense within, know when you are free from idolatry or any negative influence over you. It may take a long time, or it may seem miraculous, to feel the Peace, and Joy given by the Holy Spirit when you experience your own "Equality" or Blessings Within.

Whether you are male or female, weak or strong. Big or small, you are an Equal Human Being, created in God Image for an equally good Godly purpose.

Making it possible to confirm God's Words from those of worldly ways. Jesus spoke of this "Rebirth" * being necessary to understand spiritual matters and to be able to enter Heaven here, or after this life.

John 3:3-8; and in I Peter 1:23.

GOD OUR MOTHER TOO!

Psalm 18:30 tells us only God's Ways are perfect, a shield for all who look for help, we have been under the illusion that men's ways are the Godly way, even when they discriminate against the female half. God is not a god of partiality or inequality. Males in control added a parable by Ahab I a king who had a Prophecy Messiah, about 500 BC that there would be a coming Messiah, it was put into Genesis between the two Priestly versions of Creation that say both male and female created in God's Image. The parable story about the first people Adam and Eve sin they passed on to all offspring. Ahab was living in a society that was sexist and wrote his parable to tell about first people's sin to blame it on the woman and a talking snake!

Our growth here on earth is not only a physical growth but a lifetime of spiritual transformation from what we are were yesterday to what we have the potential to be, to come back to what God created us to be! Equal Partners, friends, soul mates!

We learn from the mistakes we make, or others have made. In the suffering lessons of making such mistakes, we can learn to do it right, equally fair and just.

Moral organizations are not exceptions. Such as Christianity at first considered illegal was persecuted for the first 300 years by those in power. It then became its own world power as the only legal religion of the Roman Empire about

325AD, for well over 1000 years, with only males in power and with inequality became at least partially corrupted.

During the first 300 years after the resurrection of Jesus before the Bible was completed in Rome, often persecuted Church met mostly within homes where the women with God's Holy Spirit to guide and confirm were treated of equal value, having experienced at Pentecost the Holy Spirit together with the men.

Most of the many followers of Jesus had before been the oppressed, the poor who experienced healing in body, mind, or spirit with many slaves, all races and sexes considered as equal children of God.

In the Holy Land when I was there in 1986 women still could not go inside the male section of the Synagogues or Mosques, behind curtains or windows they could hear, but not enter.

When Christianity became the approved Religion of Rome, under the Emperor Constantine whose word was law, only males were allowed to be ordained as Priest and only male Deacons, and male servers, were allowed beyond the rails.

Shutting off women from the Altar, not able to be Ordained began the Christian Discrimination against the female half, women gained the right to vote in America in 1921. Not officially considered in the Hierarchy of The Catholic Church until Vatican II, when many within the male Priestly orders were found to be in sexual sins. Not until this last world council of Vatican II, in 1965, did Bishops set down in their Pastoral Constitution the need "to end discrimination, for both race and sex, as not the will of God". Christ as being in the female as well as in the male. * Galatians 3:28.

The Church needs to hear now from those who can see the need and willing to stop supporting the inequality, by letting their moral leaders know, especially the Pope as the official Overseer of the largest Christian group, that does influence many in the world who want an moral excuse to justify their own continuing inequality!.

Those who can confirm need to send an appeal to Pope Francis, at Vatican City, in Rome, Italy, 00120. Takes three stamps for a U.S. letter or card.

It would be ten years after my own Spiritual 'rebirth' with God's Holy Spirit, before I would hear about Vatican II. After feeling a strong need to come back to doing God's Will in my youth. To become aware of my own more selfish will, as humans cannot possibly be as smart or know as much in the flesh as the Creator of all.

I needed at that time to know of a personal reality of God beyond my own experience of seeing a stronger supernatural Godly Hand as a 5 years old child. And over 25 years later to again experience and never doubt again of God's Presence. This time I would not see God's Hand, just know God and hear God's Voice speak the one Word of "Equality".

No question of it being God it was the word heard of "Equality" that conflicted in my mind with the then debates in Congress and often in the News, Radio and TV of the evils of communism in Russia and "Equality" being a part of such beliefs?

We were being bombarded in propaganda of equality as an enemy of a free for all Capitalist System. Not until I sought answers in the Gospels and realized Jesus and his people had lived with each other as equals, each sharing according to one's needs for at least the first 300 years of Christianity before they had been taken over by Rome, even to sharing your extra coat with someone who didn't have one.

The world's way of 'might makes right" is to take, indeed in many ways, but Christ taught it is even better to give than to take and we would be able to receive spiritual riches stored in Heaven with such giving *! Even be felt in your heart during this life! * Matthew 6:19-21

Realized God was leading me to join The Catholic Church because of their having only one Pope to reach, who then would make the needed moral decision, either to continue to discriminate against the female half, or to help end an unfair economic, political control system, by ending inequality for the female half. He is a recognized, even by unbelievers a Worldly Moral Judge.

The Prophecy of "Equality" has been given as the best time needed now to end discrimination for the female half of God's Image, to balance the inequality and injustice that may determine whether we will have a World War III or not!

Over 100 Religious Women, were the first, to go witness at the Vatican in Rome, soon after the Vatican II Counsel in 1965. To Pope John Paul I, the first Pope selected after Vatican II, to appeal an end to Discrimination within The Church. The Vatican II's message from God's Holy Spirit! He gave them an audience and told them he would do what he could. Later was heard saying to aides, He realized the Vatican Bank needed cleaning up too! Three days later He was found dead.

There is much evidence it was by the hand of evil working within the Church for where is evil going to try to work the hardest to mislead minds. God does not normally interfere with human free will choices to do good or to do evil, even among the religious. A report of a part empty glass by His bedside table of orange juice, disappeared soon after His already cold body was found in the morning. Indicating He had died early. Arsenic poisoning has no taste when mixed with juice, and no autopsy would be allowed, or on any of the former Popes at their death.

Why most evils are allowed in this world, and others are only rarely miraculously prevented? We do know God normally allows us Free Will to do evil, rather than control us like robots. Free Will being one of our most precious Holy Spirit gifts in our spiritual "Rebirth", of being able to know God's Better way to treat ourselves and each other!

God is able to help us turn the worse into something better, but not until there are enough willing to allow The Holy Spirit to work within them in the faith of God's Perfect Holy Love.

Most of those first 100 Religious women, did not get help in their day. In the generation since then, we have seen a new awakening of "Equality" in all forms of world's equal rights, in education, politics, economics.

Many now have the opportunity to see the better way for the good, as well as seeing the world's cruelty, to find the justice without, we must first start within spiritually to become more of the better we seek.

To Love ourselves, Love others, to stand up for our rights to not support the inequality that is keeping us down!

> "Christ uses no Body but Ours
> No Hands or Feet on Earth but Ours,
> Yours are the Eyes that look with Compassion
> on this World, Feet that Walk to do Good,
> Yours are the Hands that Bless
> You are the Body of Christ on earth...."

> St. Theresa of Avila 1515-1582

St Theresa, like many women felt the call from God to be a Priest but was refused by the males in the Church then, as women are now, by men's practice of inequality. The addictions of all kinds of power, selfishness, and greed, in males and in a few females too, with an inordinate need to think of themselves as better or superior!

Sometimes using threats, violence, even murder to those who would try to be what they felt were their right too.

For centuries men and women have suffered from the abuse of the ungodly, seduced or tempted by controlling powers in the world, some by forsaking their Godly purpose! Only by the Power of the Sacrifice of Jesus and Mary's Yes to do God's Will, has the debt of sin been paid, for those willing to repent and turn towards the best for all.

Closing minds, and hearts to the harm and the hurt of others, is a big part of the blindness resulting from the practice of Idolatry! The worship of a false male/only Image of God are at the root causes of many of today's inequalities. Idolatry one of the first of the Mosaic Ten Commandments. We are not meant to worship a false image of God, as we each share within us, some degree of the combined male or female Image of God. *Genesis 1:27; 5:1.

As humans we remain imperfect in this life, and are not to consider ourselves equal to God, but equal to each other, living as human children in Christ. Jesus reminds those who would follow his better way, to worship God in Spirit and in Truth. *John 4:23

Those with not hurting, or undamaged good hearts will recognize "Equality" as better than the present inequality, not only for the female half but better for males as well. Hard to love anyone you don't feel is an equal!

In moral, religious ways, we need to level first, to have the moral grounds for opposing the inequality in the unequal economic field. This is unfair to most males and even more so to most females. Prophecy is primarily given to avoid the worse we are in, or near! The Prophecy of "Equality" given both to Bishops as well as to laity in Vatican II, Pastoral Constitution, spelled out in article 29 + others. To give us a rare opportunity, good chance now for years of Peace, if

74

we are willing to practice Equal Rights for all, "Equal Opportunity" for all the People, not just for a few! To insure "Equality" for All.

If we are not willing, repent of inequalities and false idolatries, we will continue toward endless wars and eventually a nuclear World War III for billions, most of them innocent?
As life is in a fallen world because of sin and listening to a negative god instead of the best kind of a Loving God.

Jesus in Matthew 7:7, tells us to keep asking in prayer for what we need. For our Blessings Within, as well as Blessings Without. Including in verse 12, those willing to choose to live by the Golden Rule, those found within most religions and especially those with good hearts.

Equality being the essence of the Golden rule to treat others with equal fairness, as you would most want to be treated! Equality being better than inequality, just as Freedom is better than slavery. To be able to see this now, in our times depends on where you have allowed your Heart to be.

So important, necessary to ask, to seek your own personal relationship with God's Holy Spirit. Not with just any Spirit, but with the Best possible. After I heard of God's Word of "Equality", I began to realize Equal Respect, Equal Rights, Equal Opportunity, are really the essence of the Golden Rule message found in all the major beliefs and a way to Confirm, when we are not sure, what is good and best for all.

Specifically, I felt led to witness to The Pope, for His Words are heard worldwide and what He says becomes a moral example to not only believers of all kinds but can also be a moral example to non-believers as well!

It took me several years of feeling led to join The Church to actually join, as their beliefs of inequality were still being practiced, but true in most male/

only run religions. Because patriarchal languages were used to create the false thinking of God as just male by using only male nouns, pronouns, and having only males in control! At first felt I would be able to find ways to witness. Yet now after many years of trying, realize have only had or seen a token response and it is going to take many to reach the Pope, and many more not being willing to support discrimination and inequality anymore.

Not knowing at that time what else I could do, and more and more just wanting to leave sexist and negative attitudes, to hopefully find more receptive minds and to worship with people who did believe in "Equality".

Knowing God had led me to witness there, yet feeling I had tried and failed, with no way left to try. In that frame of mind, walking to the Church one morning, got less than a half block away, when I strongly felt there was no way I should go in and determined not to go there again.

Actually, turned around and walked away in the opposite direction, when I suddenly felt God's Hand in mine, with no one anywhere near or around me!

Knowing this was the same Presence of God, The Hand I had actually seen as a child, yet in looking down at my own hand I was still feeling God's Hand, but I could not see anything, just feel God's much Stronger Hand, in mine.

Only for a few moments, before God's Hand literally swung me back around in my tracks!! To once again walk towards the Church, with the assurance now at least, of my still being led by God's most Powerful Hand.

There would be other times I would want to leave, yet there are many things I really do like about The Church! Most of the Priest and most of the people who like me are primarily seeking to live life in a better world.

To be able early in the morning to listen, usually after first saying something to God, about my feelings or about a need, is one of my greatest pleasures, to know I am being heard to feel God's Loving gentle Presence and hear God's voice within my mind, as God responds with intelligence and knowledge I know I could not know, did not come from just my limited human thinking.

Only a few times in my life has there been such a strongly felt presence, compared with the usual gentle knowing of the Holy Spirit is Presence both within, as without everywhere, normally just peacefully felt when I turn my attention to God's Presence, always willing to be with and right beside or in us.

Knowing this calm's like nothing else and makes the day tend to pass in Peace and Joy, giving many Blessings Within.

To know there is no condemnation for those who belong to Christ, willing to follow as best we can. The Price for sin paid, forgiven by the Sacrifice of Jesus as Christ, the awaited Messiah for many centuries. Finally, by the Grace of God's Holy Spirit in a Heavenly "Father" union with the human Mary, the "Mother of God".

This other time of experiencing God's Hand, I felt much more strengthen to go back, realizing there was no other way for me, if I wanted to do God's Will.

Because we live in a world ruled primarily with inequality, until we work on the source, we are only putting band-aids on at the most, to cover up the blood and open sores of the damage inequality causes. It is time now to stop supporting inequality!

Have experienced enough to know God's ways are always smarter, knows what is best, and is better morally just as the source of The Heavenly Parent, Creator of our life would, should be.

To be in that kind of contact gives both Joy and Peace, when our wills are in harmony, with no reason why they should not be, and when you are not sure, to be able to just ask and get sufficient answers from the source!

It was when I was short on faith, or trust, that I could not seem to be able to talk with God or to get answers.

It does take faith in accepting even 'the dark nights of our souls that for some can last for years, some just for days, when things go wrong for us and does not seem to be our fault and no for sure answers seem to come.

You have to keep the faith, that you will understand but only in God's Time, that is not always or seldom in our own!

Like any good parent, our Heavenly Parent wants us to first above all grow spiritually, mature in our own free will, to most of all live with an equal concern for others, as well as our self, not be robots!

As a Perfect Parent wanting to help us grow but not at the price of taking away the precious gift of freedom of our Godly given free will. For better or worse, it is usually our choice to go towards the best possible life, not only for yourself but hopefully for all!

Each one can and does have a part in making life better for themselves, as well as for others. Do you know what your part is? Can you confirm it to be of good fruit?

If not, can you see where inequality or partiality is against the Golden Rule, or the teachings of Jesus to Love One Another, even your enemies!

My own spiritual gifts of Discernment or Prophecy have been limited to what I am specifically told by God's Holy Spirit, and most of the time only just before I absolutely need to know. If I knew more, I would maybe worry more. Worry one of those given thorns in my own side, and in wanting to value other people's privacy, I have rarely known what others don't want me to know.

I have a suspicion even God doesn't want to know, what isn't necessary for God to know! It is said whatever we ask God to forgive, it is thrown into an Ocean of forgetfulness. I like that Image, of God's kind of forgiveness.

Words that come from the heart and one's relationship with God can be helpful, they have been for me and one reason why I continue to try to share them. Our best hope is in putting ourselves in God's Hands for our needed and unknown guidance, with no other better place to be.

You may not feel that way, or you may feel as I once did of God's seemingly unfairness and inequality in this life and had to later realized it came not from God but from the wrong actions of other people and the evil in this world.

Plus, our limited view of God's Plans in time and space, the Purpose can be invisible to us! Hurt sometimes by just someone's choice in knowledge or lack of, being in the wrong place at the wrong time, even being in the way of nature's natural movements and sometimes fury.

Times when I was so taken with the needs and troubles of my own, I took steps backwards, in the spiritual growth we all seem to be here for. Hopefully you will avoid the worse by taking advantage of putting your own hand at all times in the care of God's Hand, by believing in your heart you surely will come out the better, not only in this lifetime but in the eternal life to come.

Are not the value of all people's life, health, and good will, worth more, than the workers profits going to only a few, profits that rightfully are best meant for the benefit of all!

EQUALITY IS BALANCING SELF CENTERNESS
TO THE UNIVERSAL GOD CONSCIOUSNESS
GOD SAID "EQUALITY"

The Southern part of North America, of the United States is my ancestrally home but have had the great fortune, even as a child, to live on different sides of America, 1000's of miles apart. To have traveled by car many times across this beautiful land, often camping out along the way.

Everyone needs to take at least one car trip across a Continent, to be able to see the diversity, not only in people and their customs, ways of talking, but in the environment how it looks and changes from state to state, as well as season to season.

Diversity is the great divider, in our world. That knowledge needs to be what awakens us, to open our eyes to tolerance, to all God Created that is so much more than just ourselves, our own ways of being are just one kind of being, among many!

Also have chosen to live in several other places too, finding every place has, at least a few special things like no other. Yet many families, friends have remained in the South, so eventually I yearned to come back to live here again, to see the progress here, of their learning to treat others who act or look different, as equal human beings now, with equal rights!

It is not just the South, there is prejudice among all people, in all places I've been. In all races among those who want to limit their world to just their kind, not realizing they are negatively limiting themselves in the process!

The more closed a society they are in, the more prejudice they tend to be! City people usually more tolerant than Country people. Then again must trade off the advantages of Country living.

The Civil Rights movement raised the moral consciousness of many, just from the natural goodness in all people's hearts, and ending a lot of former prejudice of those who are different. For most people want to do the right thing!

Yet the Civil Rights struggle for "Equality", for Equal Rights, and equal Opportunity continues, rightfully expanding now to Women's Rights.

It was not until 1921, long after slavery had ended, before the right to vote became legal for women here in America, where they would no longer be primarily just the legal property of males and many began to realize they owned their own bodies.

In some places of our world, the female half still remains the property of first the father, then the husband, and if he passes, even his brother! I remember hearing once of a young 12-year-old girl being sold by her father for $12.00. What kind of father would do that? Was he like so many others on the verge of starving, who did it just to be able to keep her from starving too? Was it to feed the rest of his family for a short time more?

Or did he just not believe in the equal human value of a female, even his daughter? Allowing the selling of another human lowers the value of all life, our concept of freedom, each one's free will, lowering it to that of cattle! Yet we are allowing it every day! There are many in all beliefs, who realize it is time to stop the thousands of years of such inequality, for political balance, as well as religious balance.

A need for equal rights, equal opportunity "Equality", to help bring out the best in all of us!
To help counter the unfair hoarding of profits, from all workers, and using natural resources that rightfully belong to all the human family!

Yet the present unjust economic system has half the world on or near starvation wages, and if allowed to continue, attempts at wage slavery will increase even more.

Because of those controlling most of the world's economy can justify their beliefs of inequality, by the continued practice of Religious inequality, while they continue to control wages and profits that result in the starvation of thousands of children every day. Millions in Hunger, and Billions more forced into low wages. Males controlling a woman's contraception, choice of pregnancy.

With the profits created by the workers, managers, consumers, beyond the reasonable expenses of doing business, needed for good living wages, and people's basic needs like health care, education, and other safety and mental needs, the safety of utility and road infrastructure are also needed too.

Instead of increasing the profits, and greed of economic controllers and political Dictators to use their power and force, as well as much of the media, such as News on Radio and TV, Movies to condition, especially the youth, but all of us, to accept the conflict, inequality that leads to war to make the youth soldiers of war and violence, instead of peace helpers!

Still many of our good customs, traditions, have been evolving for the better since more primitive times, by the outlawing of slavery, the civil rights work on racism and sexism and other forms of ending prejudice and inequality.

Few of us on a conscious level, would choose traditions that bully or belittle others.

Most of us want good relationships with others and are evolved enough to not want to see other human beings mistreated or enslaved.

Within the Catholic Church with so many different races of people, since Vatican II have been progressing towards ending racial discrimination.

Still the illogical and unfair reasons once used for slavery and racism are still being used, to keep the sexism, discrimination of the female half. Plus being a very negative moral example for those both inside and out of The Church to justify their own inequality politically, economically, as well as in personal relationships!

Adding to another form of inequality, is our more selfish political nationalism, instead of an equal concern for all people, partly due to religious differences in beliefs.

Each of us tending to think our way is the only or best way, when neither may be, when our way denies or hinders the equal rights of others.

Our Patriotism being a good example of the best we have to offer, of freedoms and opportunities we have here, so rare in many other countries. Especially the precious freedoms that stop only at the rights of others.

By using prejudice or fascist beliefs to scapegoat, the evils of inequality repeat waring cycles of violence and discord, where in the end no one wins!

We still have our free will to choose "Equality" over inequality, or beliefs in justice over injustice, and to act in ways to make them realities in this world, as well as in our hope for the next!

Do we really want to continue to bow to the negative will of so much inequality when equal Justice for all is a possibility?

Responsible Freedom is worth going towards and not away from! We will argue or debate and hopefully equally vote for what is responsible freedom. Having that equal vote is what living in Democracy is about, compared to bondage or slavery in a dictatorship.

We know the unconscious mind is formed and indoctrinated heavily by our parents and peers, also influenced by the current customs of the times, and for most of us before the age of five to seven years old it is put deep within us, and only tugs at us when our conscious mind has other competing ideas.

A natural fear of change that can be a fear of lost, of something being taken, of what is at least familiar to us. A change of anything tends to bring in an inward fear of lost, as well as what will others think, a fear of retaliation from just being or thinking differently.

Yet we are by nature a very socially loving, grouping kind of people. With a hope of a better world, a better after-life, we must be equally concerned of the cost, not only for right now but the cost in being judged by a higher court eventually. 'By what we do, as well as what we fail to do'.

Such a cost has or is being paid by a Priest, who after 49 years was stripped of his Priestly rights in The Church over his belief of the need to follow God, rather than man, in discerning a woman had a valid call from God, to be a Priest, and being willing to give the homily at her Ordination.

He was not even the Bishop who legally is needed to ordain. Just picked by the Vatican to be made an example of after his refusal to recant the Ordination. To say it was wrong, as he was expected to do, by males who right or wrong do not want to be considered less than god by anyone below them. Not willing to admit God's Will in each one can be above their own, as long as it is a well-formed and Godly Conscience!

Believing in the validity of such a well-formed conscience a good friend, the Reverend Fr. Roy could no longer ignore the confirmation from The Holy Spirit within. Believing we must above all, obey God's Will first, rather than the not always so knowable motives or limited knowledge of other humans! Even one in a position of authority over us. Other people even those in authority over us don't have the same authority as God, can't tell us to do something immoral.

Those in a right standing with God can confirm by the universal Golden Rule or by Jesus's words. God is not going to tell you to do something evil or violent to another. There are ways to confirm if our conscience is led by God or not.

After reading one of his articles I asked to include it here what he had written on Women as Priest, and he gave me his permission, being glad for others to be able to know.

The more I tried to omit some of it the more I felt led to add all of what he had sent, from my request.

Have also a postcard picture of a sweet looking little girl raising her hand at school, while standing beside her desk in anticipation, with the caption of "Who wants to be a Priest"!

Girls as well as boys do want and do need to respond to God's Calling. The majority of Catholic surveys agree!

St. Theresa of Lisieux, later named Saint and Doctor, once told her sister, as well as her spiritual director, she felt the call to be ordained into the Priesthood. The males in control of her religious order denied her, but on her death bed she asked God to be able to spend her Heaven on Earth. I like to believe her wish was granted.

I believe she is helping us now, maybe one of those 100 well trained Catholic Women who have already been Ordained by Catholic Bishops. Bishops being the only ones who can ordain a Priest and so needed now, within The Church, so short of Priest, but mostly to represent the fullness of God, as an example to our world to keep out of the sin of idolatry, of a false worship of a male only God. To end our world's inequality, the big grip the devil has to continue the violence, destruction primarily in war.

Once when I was praying and fasting in the Church after all had left. Walking around the room saying my Rosary. As I passed by a statue of St. Theresa for about the third time, looked up at her and must have looked like I needed cheering up as when I looked up she winked at me!! It was so real it spooked me out. I very slowly walked one more time and looked very carefully then left for the day and she never did it again. Nor have I ever gotten a red rose she supposedly gives after someone has asked her to obtain a favor for them and their prayers were answered. That sight still remains with me so many years ago. If I really saw that, she must really be a special Saint for someone to come down from Heaven to help us, then well Jesus did, at least that's what we as Christians believe. He was God even before coming as a human child.

Biblical Scriptures can be used to support women's authority to Preach, Teach, and Prophesy. Jesus after his resurrection, first appeared to Mary of Magdalen, one of his disciples and told her to "go and tell", can be found in John 20:17,18. Acts 2:17,18 and Joel 2:28-32 Promises that The Holy Spirit would be poured out in women too. 1 Corinthians 11:5 Women were prophesying and in Titus 2:3 with the injunction for women to teach.
Appeals to Deborah in Judges 4-6. Esther, Anna in Luke 2:36-38. Phoebe in Romans 16:1 and Triphone in Romans 16:12. And Phillips four daughters in Act 21:9 all are part of the Biblical records of women's authority to tell the Good News.

The Holy Spirits gifts listed in I Corinthians chapter12 are not limited to males. In St. Paul's spiritual maturity came to say there was within Christ, neither male nor female. We are "One in Christ". Galatians 3:28.

The Holy Spirit originally was, and many still think of as a feminine word, but like all parts of God, it includes the masculine, as well as the feminine aspects of God.

We as male and female, have both the same kind of male and female hormones in each of us, in laboratory testing, just different amounts of each male and female hormones at different times in each life. Also, the same number of ribs or bones, and organs, with some outside, some inside.

Am now reminded of another vision I had, not long after returning to the middle of California where I had been living before first going to the Hawaiian Islands. Not wanting to return, but God insisting. I had always wanted to go on a vacation to Hawaii and when I got inoculated with a deadly virus, after trying to get well for a couple of years with little success or not very long before I would come down with something from my only half working Immune System with no known cure, I asked God to let me go to Hawaii and help me find a job there for at least 6 months and that is what happened. Praise God and I seemed to be able to get better and right away got a good job in a Honolulu Hospital working nights, loving my life there I got better.

Waking up at the last of the sixth month with a reminder it was time now to leave. Each time I woke up and put it off for almost another month trying to talk God into getting someone else, I so wanting to stay on the Islands, where my health had miraculously returned. Finally, did come back to sleep in a friend's extra bedroom. Not knowing for sure whether I was to stay there, or go where? After a few mornings woke up realizing I was to leave that very day but still not knowing in what direction?

No longer rebelling, I started to take a few boxes out across their back yard to the van, I had left in their garage by an alley and back across their mostly empty, fenced in back yard to get a few more things I had.

When turning back after the 2nd load to cross again their back yard to the house, saw what I thought at first was a real live Angel (but no seeable wings), also realized there was nothing below the Waist! With only space between the ground that I could see through, but a very real looking human top part of His Body, what I believe now was Jesus! At the time my mind went to St. Michael.

Wearing a very fine, white robe with a gold sash, just to the waist, for there was nothing that could be seen below the waist!

Yet standing only five or so feet away, and just a little above my height, but with no legs, or feet! I had always thought of Jesus as being very tall.

I felt no fear, only a great Awe. His beautiful smile, yet His lips never moved, but inside my head I could hear a Godly voice telling me to go to San Diego. Then after a few moments of talking to me in my head, as I stood in silent Awe, not even wanting to move and no fear, then He just vanished, as I was just staring at such a sight.

Would live for ten years in San Diego, just a few blocks from a Catholic Church, that was open during the week where I felt led to go often to pray, then and after three years of much study joined, feeling it was both God's Will and how I would be able now to reach many with the Prophecy I had been given of "Equality" because of their having only one Primary Pastor, The Pope, for so many Christians in the world, over a billion I heard to try to reach and convince.

I first had to find a place I could afford, but wanted one near enough to the Ocean to be able to hear the waves, feeling they would remind me of God's Power, and would later find one on the Leeward side of St. Michael's Bay, a rundown but cheap at that time, little cabin next to the Pier. So, for many years convinced the vision must have been from the Angel St. Michael. Even later found a little statue of St. Michael at a yard sale that kind of looked like one of my favorite Priest there and still is, a St. Michael in many ways. A very busy real-life human Angel.

Another, reason I was then thinking it was probably the Angel St. Michael, was because this Priest I heard has many relatives who are also Priest, Monsignors, Sisters, active religious within the Church!

This last morning in early May, a friend handed me a little book before our prayers in the Chapel, on the message of Fatima.

While reading of one of the three Children, St. Bernadette as she is known now, her name was actually Lucia wrote of her vision of Mary, the Mother of God Christians call Jesus The Christ. The place where they saw the visions, now about a hundred years ago, is where the fountain of Louvres still is and where many miracles came to be.

Turning to read of her seeing her last Vision in her life, as a Nun, the little book also shows the picture of her vision. How she saw Jesus hanging on a Cross, Mary standing under the Cross on his right, with God as The Father above the Cross, But only to his waist! Then you see the Holy Spirit Dove as the Feminine or other Half of the Father God, both above Jesus on top of the Cross.
So hard to put into words the Trinity, to understand or explain how God's Spirit can be One and yet God's Nature having the attributes of both Father, Mother and Child and each able to be in all places at all times!

At Church and in prayer we say Father, Son and Holy Spirit. Representing Jesus as Child of The Mother, Father God. But because of our now patriarchal language only male nouns and pronouns are used and Mother is replaced by Holy Spirit. Yet we were created to represent the Trinity Image of One God as well as a Family of Godly people!

In the vision the human physical form of Jesus on the Cross crucified, with Mother Mary pictured at his right. Both as Divine Holy Adam and Eve's. Now both born free from sin as needed for humankinds perfect Sacrifice for sin.

LAST SECRET OF FATIMA

Reprinted from the little book "The Message of Fatima". The Ave Maria Institute, Washington, New Jersey 07882.

IN THE LAST SECRET OF FATIMA SISTER LUCIA GAVE THIS VISION TO HER BISHOP &THE POPE OF THE NATURE OF GOD AS FATHER/ MOTHER/CHILD.

Notice the Dove right above the Cross above Jesus, his human Mother Mary at his right. The Dove symbolic of The Holy Spirit, Divine Mother, with the Father Image split in half at the waist.

All Real Attributes of the One as Spirit not limited like our physical nature but primarily in Spirit form while we are primarily in this world material.

Christians call this Spiritual Family of God as "Trinity". Known as Omnipresent able to be everywhere, at the same time and all knowing. Beyond our individual physical natures while in this life, and beyond just our physical minds ability to fully comprehend.

Mary and Jesus both being Human and Divine, Create the Christ Child for a Holy and Perfect Godly human Reparation to be the perfect sacrifice for all people's sin what sinful humans could not do, make a Perfect Godly Sacrifice to remove the sin of the first humans 'Adam and Eve' passed on to their offspring in their spiritual death.

Both Mary and Jesus accepted by The Church as being free from sin from birth, and remaining so, while both being tempted as all humans are, yet remaining perfectly free of sin, needed for the perfect sacrifice, freely offered to free us from the bondage and eventual Spiritual death caused by human sin.

By Grace humans have been given a way out of the law of death from sin, by accepting the free sacrificial gift from God as Our Heavenly Father, Mother, and Jesus, provided for any who want and willing to accept in repentance for forgiveness freely given. Best now to go in Thanksgiving, Joy, Peace, and Goodwill, away from inequality in our relations with each other!

God's Hand came to me as a child, and many years later in a vision of Jesus while walking with some things to my van after waking and being told in my mind to leave that morning. Still not knowing in what direction was coming back to the house when I saw only the top half of what I thought at first was an Angel, so Angelic was His face, highlighted by a most beautiful smile. His lips never moved as I heard in my head to go to San Diego but saw no wings or anything but the grass below his waist! Later evidence of this being Jesus by what He told me while I stared in awe.

Unable to speak until He suddenly vanished. God is certainly capable of appearing in any physical form, as Jesus did for forty days after His Resurrection, before seen assuming into Heaven by many in the Mount of Olives.

Jesus had many women among his disciples, who in public were limited but then considered as equals among most of the members of Jesus, especially after the coming of The Holy Spirit, to know the fullness of Truth.

In the 3:28 Galatian teaching of all being One in Christ, no male or female, slave or free, was for the first 300 years after the resurrection of Jesus practiced among the members until the Council called by The Emperor in Rome, in 310-320 AD.

Over about five-ten years only males were allowed to create the Bible. What would go in the New Testament 'Covenant' for Gentiles as well as Jews, by added the already written Jerusalem Covenant of the earlier Mosaic Jewish people, when brought out of slavery.

Under the Emperor in Rome he declared the Bible as the only legally required religion for over the next over 1500 years.

When Christianity became the approved Religion of Rome, public Churches were first built, where in the first 300 years of Christianity they had been outlawed, only met in hidden places, member's homes and the garden of olives tomb, of the rich man Nikodemus where Jesus had laid and can still be visited just outside the Damascus Gate of The Old City in Jerusalem. Cared for now by the Church of England.

Here members still meet for The Lords Supper on Sundays, in Remembrance of Jesus and his teaching, as He had told them to do. In such danger and more like an extended family it may have been easier than in Rome to think of all as equal members of Christ body. It is also now open during the week

To even go into the large all-white crystal tomb like cave.

When Christianity became the only legal religion much of Rome became members for political, business, or social reasons, but not so easily believed, as a better belief than the ones they already had. So many did not really convert to this new Religion. All were considered separate from the already Ordained Priests, and Altar Rails were erected with only ordained males allowed in and communion given only to those who would confess to a Priest of their faith in The Church and lack of any grave or mortal sin.

The Church has continued that male only Ordination but not for the female half. The male Bishops being the only ones to decide if one had a calling to the Priesthood or if it was God's Will. In spite of evidence of God continuing to call as God Wills, not as man wills.

The Bishops called by The Pope for a world council about every hundred years. Together they ask in the council for God's Holy Spirit. Each time resulting in more of the fullness of Truth as Jesus had promised would be revealed.

In the last world council of Vatican II, in 1965, the Bishops were given the Message from The Holy Spirit for The Church to end their Discrimination for either race or sex…as not the will of God"! *Pastoral Constitution, Article 29+ Ending Racism has not been as difficult for The Church to end as Sexism.

Soon Pope John Paul II would become the first Polish Pope, instead of the normal mostly Italian Popes, up to that time. Allowing women to be Priest is still being resisted.

It remains the Pope's official decision as the Overseer of the morality of over a billion believers, still the largest Christian Religious group that has and does influence much of the morality of the world as well as the moral justifier in world political and economic control, that continues inequality for the female half of God's Image!

Mostly by misusing the Biblical Parable (not to be taken literally) meant only to tell of an eventual Messiah, and only later added around 500 BC in vs. 4 between the two Priestly Creation stories of Genesis 1:27 and Genesis 5:1. that repeated both male and female created in God's Image!

The King Ahab I 's version is a different kind of symbolic creation story, when compared to the fullness of the original Priestly version, of Adam created first, then a rib taken from the male to form a female. Yet no rib is missing from the male, same number as same of all other parts of both male and female.

We have a need for the recognition to end female inequality by our present Religious leaders, for an end to Patriarchal language and only male made laws. The God Ordained equality of both male and female, if we are ever going to be able to make peace, end the more aggressive male wars. Even more so for our Peace within, as well as without! To be "BLESSED WITHIN".

We now know males and females both have significant amounts of both male and female hormones, in each one, that varies during different times of each life, but most prominent in reproductive years.

In the majority of males there are primarily male sexual hormones and equally more female hormones in most females, but both sexual kinds of male and female hormones are in each sex, just more in masculine natures if your primarily male, and more feminine hormones if your primarily female!

This is a scientific fact that can easily be verified by most biologist and others familiar with the functions of the human body. I first realized this by working for many years as a Medical Technologist in both Biology, Hematology, and Chemistry in both Hospitals and Medical Clinics.

We are just not that different. Sexual organs of the male are only outside extensions of the body, the corresponding organ of the female is inside. Called the vagina, ending in the Womb.

Where we are most different is in our temperaments, and in gender conditioning. This greatly affects our ability to negotiate peaceful settlements and why women as negotiators are equally badly needed.

Men are by nature more aggressive, more easily hot headed, and competitive. Women by their nature usually have much less of those kinds of masculine hormones of males. Help needed of best peaceful capabilities, to be successful for all parties concerned, in all negotiations!

Eventually I was led to join The Catholic Church realizing God wanted me to witness there, partly because of their having only one Pope to reach, who needs now to make the moral decision whether to continue to discriminate against the female half, or to help end the world's inequality!

Even helping to determine whether we will have more World Wars. This time with nuclear capabilities of putting us back into the dark ages!

For the turned away from God, evil Angels are headed by Lucifer also called Satan, still in conscious control of many world leaders, many are not aware they are serving evil by their beliefs of perpetuating inequality.

From a population of over a billion humans, only a few, Less than 1-2 % are known to be in control of about 80-90% of the economic world's wealth, allowing the other 10% of all profits to be used by 98% of the rest of the people.

Most goes to the top 10 CEO's managers and business owners, good salesmen working on high commissions.

Much lesser incomes for the majority of workers who have used most of their energy and time to produce all that wealth for just a very few in comparison.

The natural wealth and resources God created for all of us, meant for the benefit of all, not for just a few!

Excessive interest rates are a result of the sin of Usury, to help make the 1% ever richer with ever increasing profits from the poor who do not have enough without borrowing because of many unfair and low wages in proportion to the profits they are making for the investors.

It was my experience in nine years of marriage to a City Planning Director, that even people in higher income brackets find it necessary to spend much of their allotted monthly incomes to be able to 'Keep up with the Joneses' so to speak, in social roles where they are expected to buy bigger better homes, clothes, cars, vacations, an inexhaustible amount of pressure to spend what they earn. Later if living to retirement, they do benefit greatly by their higher earnings in retirement plans, even higher Social Security benefits but not if they are forced by health or just want to retire early, or when the stock market drops in cycles but hopefully does not fall too drastically under their chosen chips.

The basic necessities for all needed life, of food, health care, a chance to go to school to at least learn a skill, should come from the great excess of profits of those who have much more than what they need to live high on the hog comfortably. Such as those who make more than $500,000 a year. Depending on degree of inflation, need to pay their share of taxes to even out the poorest for just the basic needs of life.

Better than taxes, profits should be more fairly or equally shared between investors, workers, and the needs of the community, nation, world for just and a fair basic living expense for those either unable to work, needing schooling, training and health care.

In this way people who are able to work will be able to get more than just survival wages, so most will prefer to work. Right now, the world's Majority, many millions in many countries do not made enough each day to keep those with families from hunger.

Thousands of children are still being allowed to starve each day, and literally millions go to bed hungry each night. It needs to stop and could be if the now 90% of the extra profits are more equally shared!

Yet, it will not stop, without the belief of what God is saying about "Equality" or Equal Rights. By creating opportunity for many in so many ways, to live and thrive, in the long run would benefit us all and take away so much fear and selfishness, that results in criminality we all randomly suffer from.

Support equal rights, equal opportunity, working towards an ending to inequality, discrimination, racism and sexism.
One Person, One Vote to justly represent the People. Preferably a government of elected judges with local, state, national and international congresses would be best to make and keep laws as needed, with elected local, national and international representatives. Judges instead of Controllers or Dictators who too often play at being above the law, instead of for the common good. Many will not judge themselves when there is no one to oversee them. A possible overseer committee, like our Senators have once they are elected.

Community could vote to send a male or female State representatives as overseers, then at a State level send two to a National and International level of independent overseers possible for best kind of Grand Jury kind of oversight.

In the recent years of our history it seems evil is trying another way to control and eliminate as many as possible besides nuclear war. By finding a way to change the DNA of our food seeds, to changing the nature of the seed to not only make it sterile, but when it is being grown near crops of natural or organic seeds to make them sterile too. Gradually being able to not only own but change the nature of food!

So far Genetically Modified Organisms, GMO's have learned to sterilizing food seeds, have been changing the DNA with carcinogens and other toxic chemicals to be not only own, and increase the cost of food but it is not helping but hurting our health with their chemicals and sterilization of seeds and there may be some truth to some wanting to cut population from billions to millions, and more to better control those left under an endless wage slavery of essential workers and Royal Players

People must be willing to act while there is time, by first confirming with the best within you, with The Creator of all. This is possible only when you are free from sin! If you are not, ask honestly to be, and keep asking until you know it is not a negative spirit answering but The God of All, a Holy Spirit of Love, who is not only Alive and Well, more Powerful, more intelligent, than us as humans are.

God will not answer until you are truly sorry, repentant, willing to forgive not only those who have hurt you, as well as forgive yourself, to make amends where possible for those you have hurt!

Able to help us turn the worse into something better, yet not until we will allow The Holy Spirit to work within us first, for our own Peace and Goodwill towards all.

WHY WOMEN SHOULD BE PRIESTS

By Roy Bourgeois

As a young man, I felt God's calling me to be a Catholic Priest. I was ordained in 1972. During my ministry I met many devout Catholic women who told me about their call by God to be Priest. After much study and prayer, I came to the conclusion that excluding women from the Priesthood defies both faith and reason.

DIGNITY AND EQUALITY

As Catholics we are taught that men and women are created equal. "In the image of God" (Genesis 1:27). Women and men are equally endowed with intellectual and moral capacity, but historically women have been suppressed and demeaned as inferior.

In a 1995 letter, Pope John Paul II stated: "Our ability to recognize [women's] dignity, in spite of historical conditioning, comes from the use of reason itself, which is able to understand the law of God written in the heart of every human being." *[1]

Yet Church leaders themselves often rationalize unjust customs that serve their self-interests, including gender inequality.

As theologian Elizabeth Johnson, CSJ, has pointed out: "Christianity took shape in the culture of the Roman Empire…. Patriarchy (rule of the Father) is a pyramid-shaped arrangement where power is always in the hands of a dominant man or group of men. As leaders adopted this pattern for its own internal life." *2 This top down, all-male clerical structure is still in place. Women are denied access to the Priesthood; nuns are scolded for not taking direction from their male "superiors." *3

VOCATION AND ORDINATION

John Paul II stated in Ordination Sacerdotalism (On Reserving Priestly Ordination to Men Alone) that excluding women from the Priesthood accords with God's Plan. *4 By contrast, in 1976 the 17-member Pontifical Biblical Commission had voted unanimously that the New Testament does not settle whether women can be ordained Priest. Theologian Hans Kung declared, more strongly: "Rome … [bases] the exclusion of women Priests on the idea that God is the "Father" and Jesus is His Son, there were only male disciples, etc. They are defending a patriarchal Church with a patriarchal God." *5

I agree. While Jesus chose twelve men to be his apostles the four gospels do not say anything about Jesus ordaining anyone. It also is not obvious that the twelve were the only apostles (John Paul II's main premise). Scholars have discovered women who served the early Church as bishops, priest, and deacons. In Romans 16:1,2 St. Paul praises Phoebe, a deacon, for her leadership. In Romans 16:7 he identifies Junia and her husband as "outstanding Apostles." *6,7

And consider Mary Magdalene, one who stayed with Jesus during his crucifixion. She also was the first to witness his Resurrection. * 8 Jesus then commissioned her to bring the good news to the male apostles who were hiding behind locked doors. She became known as "the apostle to the apostles."

Finally, a woman was chosen to bring Jesus into the world.
I – and many Priests I know -- see Mary as the first Priest. As one student pointed out: "Who is more qualified than Mary to say the words that male Priest say during Mass: 'This is My Body. This is My Blood'?"

I agree with Sr. Elizabeth Johnson that ".… Scripture shows that both in his early life and risen life, Jesus Crist included women in his community, not as subordinates to men but as sisters to their brothers.…" [9]

Despite patriarchal times Jesus surrounded himself with women of faith who went on to serve his Church in a ministerial capacity as able as the men.

The call to be a Priest comes from God. The Catechism of the Catholic Church states: "No One has a right to receive the sacrament of Holy Orders. Indeed, no one claims this office for himself, he is called by God." [10]

Many women say that God is calling them to be Priest. Who are men to say their call from God is authentic, but God's call to women is not? As the catechism says, no one can "claim" the office of Holy Orders because only God can issue the invitation. How then can men deny another's invitation? Who are men to reject God's call of women to the priesthood?

We do not exclude anyone because of race or sexual orientation. (Many Priests and Bishops are gay.) Why do we exclude someone from the Priesthood because of her gender? This rejection of women by men has nothing to do with God, but with privileged men who fear losing their power.

PRIMACY OF CONSCIENCE, PROPHETIC OBEDIENCE

John Paul II declared that there should be no debate about the ordination of women. The prohibition against female ordination "is to be definitely held by all the Church's faithful." [11]

For Catholics this is problematical. Conscience is sacred because it is our direct lifeline to God. Conscience gives us a sense of right and wrong and encourages us to do the right thing.

Even Cardinal Josef Ratzinger, before becoming Pope Benedict, affirmed the primacy of conscience: "Over the Pope…there still stands one's own conscience which must be obeyed before all else- if necessary, even against the requirement of ecclesiastical authority." [12]

The consciences of many devout Catholic women compel them to say that they cannot be silent and deny their call from God to the Priesthood. Roman Catholic woman priest Patricia Friesen explains:

In the older worldview, obedience was understood as doing what you were told by those in authority, but obedience is not doing what you are told by anyone else unless you are a child. Obedience – for adults – comes from the Latin ob-audire, attentive listening. [13]

Further, Friesen says the faithful are called to listen to one's own "formed conscience" and heart, to "the signs of the times," and to the Spirit.

Other Roman Catholic women priest, over 100 now like Friesen, refuse to be cast out by excommunication, declaring:

We are loyal members of the Church who stand in the prophetic tradition of holy obedience to the Spirit's call to change an unjust law that discriminates against women. We are obeying well-formed and well-informed consciences.

We want balance, a more holistic image of God, renewal. Unity in a community of equals where all are welcome at the table.... *14

I believe the debate about ordaining women in the Catholic Church comes to this: Who can hear the Word of God? Who using faith and reason, can "understand the law of God written in the heart of every human being"? *15

The late theologian Edward Schaerbeek wrote that the Holy Spirit is not heard or served well by an "authoritarian" Church government. Rather the whole of the people of God" can channel the Holy Spirit. *16

Clearly the Holy Spirit is working through these prophetic women. Our faith community is overcoming our patriarchal conditioning to truly respect women as equals. The ordination of women in the Catholic Church is rooted in Love, Justice, and equality, and is inevitable. Signed Roy Bourgeois

NOTES

1 John Paul II, 1995, "Letter of Pope John Paul II to Women."
2 Elizabeth Johnson, April 22, 2014, "Jesus and Women: 'You are set free,'" Part I, in Global Sisters Report, a project of the National Catholic Reporter. Congregation for the Doctrine of the Faith, April 2012, "Doctrinal Assessment of the Leadership Conference of Women Religious."
3 John Paul II 1994, Ordination sacerdotal is.
4 Hans Kung, July8, 1991, "The Christian Thing to Do," Newsweek interview with B. Ivey.
5 Bridget Mary Meehan, 2008, "There Have Always Been Women Priest," the Association of Roman Catholic Women Priest.
6 Dr. Dorothy Irvin has researched archeological evidences of Women ministries in the early Church.
7 Elizabeth Johnson, May1, 2014, "Jesus and Women: "You Are Set Free," Part II Elizabeth Johnson, Part 2
8 Catechism of The Catholic Church, Section 1578.
9 John Paul II, Ordination sacerdotal is.
10 Herbert Vorgrimler, ed., 1969, Commentary on the Documents of Vatican II. Volume 5: Pastoral Constitution on the Church in the Modern World, 134.
11 Patricia Friesen, 2008, "A New Understanding of Priestly Ministry: Looking at a Church in Crisis," in Women Find a Way:
12 The Movement and Stories of Roman Catholic Women priest, eds., E. H. McGrath, B. M. Meehan, and I. Ramming, 31-32.

13 Elsie H. McGrath, Bridget M. Meehan, and Ida Raming, eds., 2008, Women Find a Way: The Movement and Stories of Roman Catholic Women priest

14 John Paul II, "Letters of John Paul II to Women." Edward Schilebeck 1990, Church, The Human Story of God

15 See also: Jules Hart, 2011, film Pink Smoke Over the Vatican, http://www.pinksmokeoverthevatican.com

16 2013 My Journey from silence to solidarity

MORE BLESSINGS WITHIN

Most of us have grown up in worldly beliefs of inequality. Men from birth are more often given a sense of superiority, while the female half historically has tended to be thought of as not as important and often pushed aside in mental, emotional, if not physical ways.

Beliefs of "Equality" help go towards more Peaceful relationships.

Even through males and females each have both male and female kind of sexual hormones, as well as many other kinds of hormones that keep us growing, feeling alive and even motivated.

We need the primary female hormones mostly within the feminine nature to find ways to cooperate, negotiate with others. Working with common ground to help balance the more combative, aggressive hormonal nature of males to help prevent more violence, make amends for past harms for peace instead of revenge!

Not by force or violence for that, as soon as possible is turned into more forms of getting even. For many reasons we need a balance of male/female equality in our beliefs and religious systems to flow out into our political, even economic fields.

"Equality", the Prophetic Word God gave me at my "Spiritual Rebirth". Rebirth Jesus taught in the Gospels of John 3:3, we all need to experience and when we do will receive at least one spiritual gift such as the gift of Knowledge, Discernment, Wisdom, Healing and other such Wonderful Miracle gifts from Heaven. Help we need to create heaven here on earth.

Quietness is the place to hear God's Voice. Beginners will need a quiet place to still their minds, to learn to carry God's Peace and Joy, the stillness within you.

"I AM WITH YOU, I am with you, I-am-always-with-you. Those too earthbound, find it hard to hear in their hearts, the ever-present Heavenly Bells of the Shepherd.

"To end discrimination within The Church, of race or sex…as not the Will of God". The Holy Spirit spoke at Vatican II, in their Pastoral Constitution Article 29+ 1965. Yet still ignored by many religions traditionally controlled only by males, either worshiping a god of inequality, or into idolatry against The Mosaic Ten Commandments. Jesus, as Christ, spoke of God as "ABBA"=our "Heavenly Parent" in the spoken Aramaic language of the Holy Land people. Includes the Nature of Mother as well as "Father" for God.

Women have suffered for many centuries from the dominance of male control, even violence by those who choose to interpret God as a god of partiality or inequality! Rationalized by literally taking a parable that was meant to be symbolic of the first people Adam and Eve's fall into sin and the need for a sinless Redeemer.

This parable was and is still used to justify customs of inequality and sexism to the female half, as well as racism or to those weaker, both male and female, in contrast to the earlier, official Priestly Versions of Creation, of the female and male both created in The Image of God.

In the "Adam and Eve Parable" inserted later and between the first and third earlier of the official Priestly stories, of the Original Biblical Creation stories.

This Parable of the human need for a Godly Redeemer. Placed between the two original Priestly versions with at the most a ~ not even that in some not as accurate translations. I had never been taught or noticed such a ~ before as meaning a new story starts, an era in time, or the beginning or end of a story. A knowing clue of what was not literal but symbolic, inserted between the first two Creation Stories when Bibles were translated from the original Hebrew and Greek into Chapters and Verses such as ~ dividing into the Chapter 2 and starting the new Ahab I version in verse 4 of Chapter 2.

The Official Creation according to our best recorded history took place over periods of times (eras) given in the most recent language translations of Patriarchy expressed as days, but the original Hebrew word for day is the same as for era, or periods of time in the simple early writing meanings. Each symbol had to stand for much as written in stone. Now we have many definitions for aspects of similar things, such as periods of time, separated into days, months, years, eras.

The Parable of Adam and Eve passing on their sin of not following God and believing evil instead, resulting in the loss of both human paradise and their Spiritual life, and was for a Human/Godly Redeemer who the people held out hope for.

Some versions of Scriptures mistranslate the female as a help-maid, instead of a helpmate. Also used in Biblically times to justify the inequality of the female half, as not equal but the property of first the Father, then the Husband and often if he died first the oldest Brother. As a way to keep the female in ignorance and bondage. She did not begin to become free in most societies until she like males, gained the right to vote to have an equal say.

One of the few Biblical definitions of God is of a God of "Equity", of "Equal Justice" "not a god of partiality" * Deuteronomy10:17+, Romans 2:11. +

To receive God's Peace within as well as without, you need to recognize a God of Equality who created an equal male and female, for equal give and take. Yet still Imbedded or never realized God's Ways of Equality, in Loving of One Another, "Even for your enemies" * Matthew 5:43 is the Golden Rule of treating all with equal respect, "Equality", as the best way to make them friends instead of keeping them as enemies.

The more you are willing to give of yourself the more you will be given and come to know the heavenly joys, of being Blessed Within. Trusting God will supply what you need for this life as you need it!
The world's evil way of riches is of ever self-consuming, bigger and better hoarding. A better way to attain heavenly experienced riches here and now, is by letting go and giving. "For you are receiving the goal of your faith, the salvation of your souls." * I Peter 1:9

Gives blessings of joy and peace within, found in no other way!
Our earth is alive with miraculous blessings giving testimony to the Presence of an Intelligence, a Creative and Loving God. In the beauty and diversity of each flower much diversity of life that can be seen in nature, let alone the variety of life from the microscopic or X-ray, all working synergistically together, to allow each a needed time and space.

Slow down your pace of life to observe and listen. To be thankful, for so much that is here to have and to share. Seek a holy concern and perspective in both thought and deed.

In going towards peace and love, know every human being needs the basic safety nets of food, shelter, a chance to become the best each has the talent, desire to be, benefiting all in the long-term, many times over repaid.

To stop the present build-up of anger, ending in terrorism of revenge from the inequality of wars, crimes against one another plus family conflict if inequality continues to rule.

Being born into the human family is enough pro-life reason for a safety net, just as taxes or tariffs are justified for our collective needs such as fire, police protection, garbage collection. Community, State, National, International protections are for equal justice needed to protect the basic rights of all.

Equality does not mean anyone has the right to anything more than each one's birthright to a basic life, liberty, and pursuit of happiness (or talents) extending to the space, or equal rights of another. Whenever possible, to be able to live without hunger, with shelter, needing learning opportunities equal to talents. We all benefit from each having the opportunity to live up to each one's possibilities!

None of us alone can do much about this without others to work with. How many dedicated people would it take to succeed at such a goal as a good minimum wage? A fair share of the profits created from the labor of workers, investors, consumers, all using the world's given by God natural resources, created for the benefit of all!

A few use the world's present profit system, so their primary money income comes from their profits obtained, while most people's incomes are based on their labor. Most workers kept at the lowest possible level by a very few holding controlling interest, stocks, in the largest International Corporations.

Less than 0.1% of 1%. most males, making the majority of the economic decisions. Deciding profits, wages, world-wide by hiring CEO's to do the will of the few who set the workloads, and scale of pay world-wide.

To accomplish this, the CEO's are paid a very great deal extra, in terms of not only a salary in the millions, and valuable stocks and other such bonuses.

An unfair economic system for 80-90% of the people, that yearly increases the profits off the backs of the worker's wages, and the consumers cost, as well as quality of the products, even increase profits by the use of inflation. All the time using limited natural resources meant for the use and benefit of all.

The profits need to be shared much more fairly, not ending up as they do now, up to 90% in the control of only a handful, in over 7 billion people!

A more cooperative or a more equal sharing of profits is needed. We need prosperity for people world-wide, doing what we can to insure a more stable and prosperous peace for all.

Some selfishly continue their beliefs of inequality, by lightly reasoning from patriarchal scriptures that seem to define God as having only a male nature and not equally female, by using only male nouns and pronouns of He, Him, His. Resulting in customs and traditions of sexism, racism.

In the longer arc of Godly Justice, the bill of injustice is coming due. For God created both male and female in The Image of God, expecting both to be treating each other with at least the equal respect of the Golden Rule.

The twisting of the Golden Rule of whoever has the gold makes the rules, or the physical 'might makes right' is not right, nor of God's Intent. Not in the interest of any in the end.

Creating an unequal imbalance. Most of the people know in their hearts they are of equal human value, even in spite of long being treated unequally.

By spiritually experiencing the Holy Spirit of God one can confirm humans, as God's children, were created to be in the Image of God and are of equal value.

What one has or seems to have more of, more is to be expected, and the more responsibility one has in doing something to help the whole!

Like the public human slave auctions, or the forced battles in the old Roman Colosseums, hopefully both have had their day. I have yet to meet anyone anywhere in near mental good health, who wants to give another their rights to a free life, to be abused, forced to do what is against their Will.

Most of us would agree that each one's rights, ends at the space of another. Especially obvious when it is in our space!

Most of us would prefer to have the right to our own lives, not to be bullied, or forced to do what is against our better judgement or free will. Even to seeing, if being honest, the need to extend that right to others.

Exceptions might be those under the care or custody as a parent, those of legal age but mentally unable to make safe decisions, as well as those legally convicted of a crime and known to be physically harmful to others.

There should always be an overlooking judge in such situations. Too much power for one involved person to have over the others, too easily misused!

With the equal respect of the Golden Rule many can realize that all people's equal rights, equal opportunity, "Equality", is worth going towards, as God's better way of equal justice.

My feelings are 'If we must fight for something, besides in self-defense, let it be for the equal rights for all'. But non-violently, and by all legal means, for to try to force others by using physical violence would be repeating the violence of inequality, used for the past many years of wars of 'physical power makes right'.

Equality or equal rights for all, cannot be pursued by seeking a physical fight or in war. Equality is a spiritual non-violent war that is won first within, by seeing the wisdom of having legal protection 'Life, Liberty and the Pursuit of Happiness', not for just some of us, but for all.

Since many of us have had some amount of conditioning by physical force to control us during childhood, if helped us become wiser we have not been too hurt by it, but for many it has been a mixed bag, and we may need to un-condition ourselves to forgive what is known and even unknown, to stop the otherwise becoming our repeatable cycle. To accept our mutual equality failings as well as good qualities, and the right to everyone's equal respect and opportunity, finding ways of releasing any bitterness, or negative-ness it may have caused us. Possibly as even most likely done in ignorance or repeating a cycle from their own inequality, once done to them.

Break the cycle, for yourself, for them, if possible, once you realize the immorality of continuing, a cycle of violence that has us morally just where we are, in one war after another of inequalities and negative revenges to each other!

We can do it! We have already begun. Especially since women gained the right to vote, in the early 1920's, in the U.S. Democratic Countries can vote in leaders who will help us legally increase our equality, by voting out those that are unequal.

Joining or creating groups to tackle a problem you've seen but can't do alone!

Those who prefer or have no choice but to live under a dictator, or religious leader who tells them, instead of God how to think, there are plenty of such places to go.
For those who cannot leave their unequal or unfair situation, you can choose to share as you grow in equal respect for your own life, as well as others, work towards helping the next generation, in at least knowledge and going towards the equality of democracy!

Don't just accept as your fate, you will lose all that way!

I felt God sent me to the Holy Land many years ago to what I thought was a Peace Vigil, which I did for three months. With a woman friend I met from New Zealand, who I realized God encouraged her to help me for three months before she had to leave. Just as we had been able to gather enough, over 5000 signatures.

Then to realize it was to also to verify for myself, by finding out about the original Aramaic language spoken at the time of Jesus, who called God "ABBA" a combination of "AB" for Dad and "BA" for Mom.

Not just the "Father" Image for God, as "ABBA" was later translated into our patriarchal male-controlled current languages, now used in most scriptures!

"Abba" literally meaning our "Heavenly Parent" in the Aramaic language Jesus used in speaking to the people. Such names for God such as the Hebrew (el) = ('l), and only later expanded to Elohim, as spoken among the Priest meaning the fullness or Family of God. Notice the little first symbol, seems to indicate the smaller female half? So many 1000's of years old no human can know for sure their intent in their beginning of the language. I would find it carved on Mount Sinai where God gave Moses the Ten Commandments, right inside the little Elijah Cave, just below the summit.

The 'Abba', Jesus used, has been kept in only two places I've found in our present-day Biblical translations, in Mark 14:36, and also mentioned by St. Paul in Romans 8:15, but when translated elsewhere in the New Testament, just the patriarchal word of 'Father' for God has been used, with the addition of using male pronouns such as He, His, Him, further conditions the mind, in thinking of God in a human male/like Image, creates the sin of idolatry a false image of God.

The Holy Land is called Palestine by the Arabs, and Israel by the Jewish people. The Holy Land was Biblically given to all of Abrahams Descendants, according to Genesis 17:7. That includes Arabs and Christian, as well as Hebrews, as both relate physically, or at least Spiritually to Abraham, God called out of the sins of idolatry.

Part of the land was specifically designated to be for the Descendants of Isaiah, the late miracle child of Abraham and his wife Sarah when both were in their old age. Now known as the Jewish People. Most Christians consider themselves too as Spiritual Descendants of Abraham, if not directly related to Jews and Arabs. And are not we all related as humans? We are separated not only by racism, but differing beliefs.

If Isaiah descendants are to have legal control of the Country of Israel, they are not to keep out those who come in Peace, or as a Pilgrimage to their own Holy Places primarily in Jerusalem and Bethlehem, or not to destroy Arab and Christian Holy places such as in the communities around Nazareth, Cana, and the Sea of Galilei.

The Jews, Arabs, and Christians have fought each other for many centuries off and on. In between times of troubles, as neighbors they have long lived together in peace, sometimes for hundreds of years with one or the other being in the minority. It seems to be mostly leaders who for their own reasons (personal control, fame, fortune), have instigated or not been willing to judge rightly the personal differences or religious conflicts.

In the past 2000 years all three beliefs have been able to live in The Holy Land in Peace, most of the time, and surely can once again if able to forgive and regain that peace.

The acceptance of God's Holy Spirit into one's heart, in the first 300 years of Christianity, helped established the teaching of Jesus, as being one of the biggest differences from the Jewish Covenant or most other religions.

Whereas before Jesus came, The Holy Spirit of God had only been given to a few prophets and/or to some of the Leaders.

Being able to have the Holy Spirit of God to live within, as Jesus promised, made it possible for them to worship God in spirit and in truth!

In John 4:24, In the New Covenant of Christianity All members were to be baptized by the indwelling of God's Holy Spirit into the willing heart of the believer. Christian Baptism by water, or even spiritual baptism in situations, such as the thief on the cross with Jesus.

When baptized as a baby, they are only able to take communion, after religious instructions and give willing consent after the age of reason, usually around seven years or later, and within a ceremony of Confirmation, to become a member with the whole Church!

Male Christian Bishops wrote the Bible around 315 A.D. in Rome adding only some of the writings they could agree on. What had over the years been written by the Apostles and disciples during the first 300 years of Church, after Jesus had been assumed into Heaven telling followers to allow the Holy Spirit to guide them, after Pentecost. To be The New Christian Covenant added to their Jewish Scriptures, already written and known for centuries, as the older Jewish Covenant.

To be able to keep a right to be there now, the Jewish people will need to keep their Religious ownership of the land, for compared to the many Arab and Muslim nations, they will by population, remain a minority. The justifiable fear of being a religious or racial minority and being voted or forced out is at the root of their present behavior at this point, it seems to me.

The backing of the stronger US and maybe UN or League of Nations is probably all that is preventing them right now from an all-out war between the much larger Arab nations that surrounds most of Israel.

Either the League of Nations should be the ones to broach a Peace Settlement, as they were the one to give the land back to the Jews after the end of World War II, for their homeland. After being so badly persecuted and decimated during world war II. Or if the League of Nations are not up to it, then maybe the U.N. and U.S, other agreeing Nations.

The compensating of the Arabs by also providing them with a homeland too seems necessary as well, for any lasting peace.

Those who are being held on the West bank from their homes and in guarded camps near the Dead Sea Desert area, near Jericho, need an International Court of Appeals to turn to. Judges for those living in the land, to be able to be assured of their rights.

The seven months, I lived in the Old City of Jerusalem in 1986, it was pretty much divided into thirds, the smaller third being the Christian area with the Christian Churches and Homes, while the other main two thirds were divided in The Old City between the Jewish and Arab sections, each bordering on two sides of the Temple Mount.

Both having their own side of the Holy Mount, within the Walled Old City. The other two sides being the two outside walls of the Old City, on the Mount of Olives side. Plenty of space for a new Temple left on this eastern side of the Holy Mount, where the Hebrew Temple of Solomon last stood.

While I was there, they were excavating Solomon's steps just above the ruins of David's City, already partly excavated, up to the now wall of the Temple Mount, that leads to the now vacant Temple area, next to the Golden Gate on the eastern side.

The Jewish people do need a homeland and believe they have been given the land by God to Abraham, his old age miracle son Isaiah and descendants, and by The League of Nations, in reparation of World War II.

So do the Palestinians also descendants of Abraham, by another women then held in bondage, and now need a homeland. Their ancestors have also been living there for centuries, most of the time in peace. We know at least for the past few centuries and have keep up the care of their own religious Holy Places, as well as did not destroy Jewish Holy places.

This land many Arabs were living there after WWII was evidently not considered or realized as a recognized nation by the League of Nations at the time it was given to Israel or did not realize there were so many Arabs actually already living there. As it was said by some of the few who had visited to be primarily a desert wasteland.
There is still a lot of desert, including especially in the area of the Dead Sea and the Sinai Desert with only mostly smaller tribes of the Desert Bedouin, who like the related Samarians are now living there and claim to have been for centuries.

Many of the smaller towns I visited, in 1985 where Jesus had been born, and grew up in Bethlehem, Jericho, Tiberias, Nazareth, Cana, are still almost all Arab, as was said to be in the other areas around Tiberias and communities across on the other side of the Galilee Sea I did not visit. Many lived in since Biblical times of Jesus. All direct descendant's, of Abraham, Arabs, Jews, Samarians, all living in The Holy Land off and on!

It is around Tel Ave, and the many other coastal, as well as inland towns on the way to the mountains of Jerusalem that are now primarily Jewish populated. Except for highly fortified like forts outpost near Arab communities.

In The book of Genesis 13th chapter, there is the story of Abram, when he first traveled into the Holy Land, in dispute, with his nephew Lot. Both with many herds of life-stock, of their herdsmen getting into arguments, so Abraham told Lot to choose to go into one direction and he would take the other part of the land, so there would be no strife between them!

Lot choose to go towards the Jordan Plain, and set out eastward. That road now starts in Jericho, down the mountains of Jerusalem and goes to below sea level at the Dead Sea, then eastward to what is now the border of Sinai desert and border of Egypt. As I needed a passport to go on to Mt. Sinai, where Moses camped in the Sinai Desert to be given the Ten Commandments, on the Mountain on their many years going to the Holy Land.

In between that area and closer to the Dead Sea is where Lot chose to settle, in what was then a well-watered land, before Archeologists suspect of many Meteorite showers, landed on or near that Sodom and Gomorrah area, causing so much destruction and many fires over the land. Believed at the time as sent from God for their sexual sins and inhospitality.

In this primarily desert land that borders the dead Sea, could see occasionally stumps or post covered in salt crystals, some that could take the shape of humans, but no towns anywhere in that area. Heard it is from the lack of water as there are only desert Bedouin tribes who continue to live in that area.

It was after Lot and his herdsmen separated to go to that area that God spoke to Abram and said: "Look about you and from where you are, gaze to the north and south, east and west; all the land that you see I will give to you and to your descendants forever." "Abram then moved his tents and went on to settle near the 'terebinth', which is at Hebron. There he built an altar to the Lord. From the Word of the Lord." *

*This is one of the three Stories of the Covenant with God, in Genesis, found in Genesis chapters 13 to18, where God speaks to first Abram, later to be called Abraham, of what part of the land his descendants, will inherit of the then land of Canaan.

A peace settlement needs to be made now between the two main parties. As it was evidently not understood by The League of Nations, the number of Palestinians who were still living then in the land, who claim Jerusalem too, as one of their Holy Cities. As for the Jewish people it is still their primary one.

Till then both will continue their dispute as an on and off war, not ending until the rights of both are recognized.

Those that were living in what they knew as the land of Palestine at the time, were promised to be adequate compensated in the agreement for the Israeli's to take over the land.

In many cases I heard of, while I was there, for various reasons many were not compensated by the Israelis, or it was felt it was insufficient for the cost of their having to move.

Others felt they had no other suitable place to go, when the Israeli Government ordered them off their land, saying it was needed for Israeli growth. Or that is what I was told by the Arabs living there then.

Many I do know were later pushed into the West Bank or in fenced in Desert camps. I saw one camp myself, driving by in a group van, about a 1/4 mile away, off on a dirt road, not far from the highway to the Dead Sea, in that direction, just a few miles outside the city of Jericho. I hear it is still there now over 40 years later!

We need to regain the recognition of equality for all, especially there now as it is within their beliefs and in the Constitution of Israel, for Peace it is necessary to become a real Holy Land again, safe for all religions, for pilgrimage as well as for tourism. Instead of a constant war zone site, it has become.

Living in the Golden Rule, what all the good teachers teach. The ethical way of good people is the caring for others, as we care for ourselves. Making it possible to have "Blessings Within" as well as "Blessings Without".

Negative emotions such as anger, revenge, hate take us away from the best kind of Love we most want to go towards because there are no negatives such as hate, envy in the Perfection of God's Holy Nature so much more and better than our limited ways!

Stories in scriptures of God being angry, are men's way or words expressing the negative cause and effects of many of our actions, the hurt to the innocent that comes from negative choices and having only human negative words to use.

Like the clay that we are created from, God is willing to help us shape, but not to make us become like robots, by taking away our free will, to be our best or less in this life, leaves it up to our expression in the culture we are put into. God's Words are in scriptures, plenty of them, but expressed within the customs and traditions of the male only writers who had to obey the only male rulers over them, as in many positions of past control of our world.

Knowing this we still can have the help we need, in the form of prayer, in confirming our Holy Spirit guidance worthy to help rebalance our internal pieces of our own work or art, song, even just our smiles to brighten, lighten one another's maybe painful day. Balancing with positive thoughts to replace the negative parts of our wholeness, as we individually seek to help each other collectively bring Blessings Within, as well as Without!

FOR GOD GIVES FOUNTAINS OF TRUTH TO THE HEARTS, WILLING TO FOLLOW THE ONE TRUE GOD CREATOR OF ALL! EQUALLY LOVING ALL!

While people can and do find many things to worship, money, fame, power, the only ONE worthy of our worship is A Godly Spirit of Holy Love. The One who like a fountain of Love can be both within us, as well as without.

AS THE NAME DOES NOT MATTER AS MUCH AS THE MEANING OF THE NAME, THE "I AM WHO AM". THE ONE WHO IS WITHIN, AS WELL AS WITHOUT!

Those who can love others, as well as themselves will want such a Heavenly Parent, both as a Mother, as well as a Father, as a Best Friend and Guide to lead even to Eternal Life.

This Spirit of Holy Love will help you to see for yourself, the value of being an equal part of the whole, in harmony with, not only your own being, but feeling that harmony with others!

Those who have been hurt can be released from those hurts, by asking God's Holy Spirit for a new heart, by a spiritual rebirth*, to be able to confirm and experience God's Holy Love yourself. *John 3:3-8.

DESMOND TUTU SPEAKS:

"People of religion have no choice in the matter.

Where there is injustice and oppression, where people are treated as if they were less than who they are - those created in the image of God - you have no choice but to oppose...that kind of injustice and oppression."

"We do our religions scant justice, we put our religions into disrepute, if we do not stand up for the truth, if we do not stand up for justice, if we are not the voice of the voiceless ones, if we are not those who stand up for those who cannot stand up for themselves."

"We inhabit a universe that is characterized by diversity.

There is room for everyone; there is room for every culture, race, language, and point of view." "Almost everywhere the rulers are out of touch with the people.

A HOLY LOVE

In the Liberating of India, Gandhi taught: "Live as if you were to die tomorrow. Learn as if you are to live forever".

Nothing on earth seems to be guaranteed in this life, for either the good or the bad, none of us have any automatic protection for anything, even when we seem to be sometimes miraculously protected, it will still be because of God's Will, not ours, and usually only for the better purpose of all, but not to be counted on, as I once thought.

Many a time I know I have been like miraculously spared, but not always at the time or in the way I thought I should have been protected.

Suffering can also be a form of testing and strengthen us for what we may have to go through and not give up on later. Part or even most of mine, belonging in that category.

A means to learn spiritual lessons and testing may be allowed to see if we are strong enough, yet not to let it kill our Spirit or make us bitter.

Even though we receive The Holy Spirit if we were baptized, as a growing child we still have to mature spiritually.

If we cannot remember having a personal experience with The Risen Lord, a confirmation with Loving One Another, even our enemies, then we may still need a "Rebirth" experience. See John 3:3

Only God can 'See' over all, know what is best, without the selfish bones we as humans tend to have, partly because of our limited sight, living mostly in a material limiting kind of life!
Yet there is nothing that can happen that God cannot then turn towards our eventual good, at least for those of us who are willing to seek to do God's better Will.

We may or may not see the results for years, possible not in this lifetime, but there is enough evidence that it will be for our benefit to 'keep the faith' of God's better plan for us!

A good way to become more aware and to grow in faith, is to be thankful for each new day, and to seek forgiveness, reparation for any wrong, as soon as you realize you have done wrong! A Godly way of aiming towards the best rather than less.

At my own baptism at 14, taking a vow of and obedience to God's Will, more trustworthy and loving than humans can be, with knowledge not available to humans in our limited human space and time.

We all have a need for such a friend, even to be able to confirm with assurance, when not sure.

Also knew it would be best for me to take a Vow of Poverty, later found out it would benefit me much more than I could have possibly realized at the time, not realizing how vulnerable my life would become, in numerous dangerous entrapments, hidden among the affairs of money that can so easily entrap us.

Maybe to keep me from being spiritually blinded, to keep my vows in spite of being sidetracked at times, with negative baits of material objects.

For the first half of my life it was no big problem as I was able to make a good salary, so the vows were of no big burden, helping me to care about others and not as much about my own material needs, to give is so much more ego satisfying than to be given.

It was mostly in the second half of my life, after my health would not allow me to keep a good paying job, or even a paying job at all a long time, the daily struggle tended then to become the keeping of enough food, a bed or safe place to rest at night.

Tempted every once in a while, to follow false gods who would promise so much more or pursue worldly things that can so easily become like gods to us.

Yet, deep down knowing nothing can compare to the only One worthy to worship, a God of a Holy Love, the giver of our life force as well as source of all good things.

During World War II in the days of my middle childhood, between 8-13 years old, anything except for barest necessities, even for the middle classes were thought of as luxuries, as much was rationed because of needs for the war.

Even in our growing up knowing many in the world did not have enough of what we at least here in America, did have. We still lived in relative peace with enough food, clothes, and the warmth of family and friends.

My parents had become adults during the worldwide 1929 depression and struggle hard for what little they did manage to have, but being believers in a Good God, they taught us to be thankful for what little we did have, and it seemed to be plenty.

My Father had been a Marine and had great pride in both his country and family but was way too strict with my younger and beloved brother who suffered from Dad expecting him to be The Man, long before his time. For Dad knew what we did not, that time on earth was very short for him because of his continuing to fail health from just a little bleeding hole in his stomach, the size of a pinhead. They would not be able to find it until his autopsy after four painful and unsuccessful operations.

Not long after my brother and I were baptized, my brother was only a little over 12, and my youngest sister three, Dad would get very sick again throwing up a lot of blood, and within days would be gone!

Everyone was devastated, especially my mom. For the first time I realized how differently I was spiritually thinking, even from our large extended family who gathered to be with us.

I seemed glad he was finally out of his pain and misery and had no doubt he was in a better place than we, being now in the actual Hands of God, I knew he was in Heaven.

When I would try to talk to them about it, or try to tell them, they would only cry more!

At my insistence spent the night before his funeral and burial, in an all-night vigil beside his open casket. Sitting beside one of my Aunts willing to go with me, partly to appease my mom as she walked painfully in her high heels the five or six blocks to the mortuary.

This inability to really listen, to even hear or accept what I had to say with any seriousness by most, I soon realized would be the norm for me.

Knowing young women were primarily to be helpful, to look as pretty as possible and most of all be good, not to cause any trouble.

It was not just from my family, it was the whole society of our times, seemingly the whole world's moral way of seeing the female half.

A statue of Venus, without a head, her arms and legs tied by man-made ropes is pretty much where I felt we as females had been so long ago tied too.

Only very gradually in my time would this "She" be able to find a way to gradually take off the ropes that had bound her knowing many still remain.

Allowed to perform as entertainers, but in real life treated too often as objects, as overworked mothers, lovers, wives, maids' nurses, secretaries, rarely seen or known seriously as equals.

Even for me trying to be a woman's voice, except at times when I wore the uniform of a Nurse, or when I later found the Lab and a whole new world of science. I quickly learned to prefer wearing a Lab Technologist coat, to still realize a women's thoughts would rarely be as equally respected as that of the man's!

But my studies and work showed otherwise, and my confidence increased. From the beginning I knew that if I were to try to tell even best friends that I had seen God's Hand as a child, few if any would be able to believe me! So spiritual things I avoided talking about then.

Some of my seriousness about God must have rubbed off as I was elected Chaplin for Job's Daughters at 15 or 16, which I loved, looking for wisdom from Scriptures to share and trying to tie it into something uplifting we could all relate too.

In so many ways I've had little reason to feel sorry for myself, and rarely have. For in many ways I know I have had such a good life, thanks to many blessings at just the most needed times and my thankfulness of being blessed with such a good loving family.

The Racism in the news recently has hurt and put down so many of the diverse racial and religious differences we have in this country I had been able to mostly avoid being white, until I moved to Hawaii and experienced for the first time the stigma of being a 'Hali'. It was good for me to experience it, maybe because it was mostly short lived and just among the locals I worked and lived with there, all of a darker skin than mine. Once they saw I was willing to work as hard as them and do my share of the job we had to do, they began to accept me as one of them.

Have also come close to death many times. Enough times of not feeling blessed at all. Because of so many close calls never thought I would make it to such an old age, yet here I am, still trying to learn to be a better writer, to be able to share what a full, blessed and beautiful life, with God being in our corner can be. Even with my health as fragile as ever.

My first desire for a vocation was to be Reporter, a real Newspaper Reporter, and thought of it as my job while working in my Junior year on our High School Newspaper, actual what was our homework for us in the class. We had a real-life Female Reporter as a Teacher and only a handful of students. She was very good and loved teaching us.

It didn't seem hard but good fun to do, so I was puzzled and surprised why I could not, when I asked God, if I could make my living writing, for in my head heard a Godly voice saying "You'll never make your living writing", as a very clear and immediate response. How true that has been. In spite of my surprise and belief I could still be able to someday become good enough.

Realize now for one thing, my love for journalism never included my boredom and impatience with English which I took only in my freshman year of high school and being it was my 8 o'clock class, slept through most of that year's classes. How I got a C in it was a surprise and much relief as I swore never to take such a class again. Bad decision, my writing has suffered since.

From then on it was just the 'Who', 'What', 'When', 'Why' and 'How' that seemed to matter to my writing and still does, but how you frame the questions and answers is where the art comes in. Plus, just knowing where to put or not to put the commas, a whole art in itself!

Now after trying to write for so long realize, if you don't get the commas in the right place it will probably be misunderstood by at least some or becomes so easily misconceived.

To finally have to realize not only that I had no natural talent, but there would be no getting through with my words to those I most needed to write for, the all-male elites in control of The Church. Still very much a part of a Worldly Roman Empire of Billions of followers, called The Catholic Church.

Eventually I would write about what I was learning, but in Diary form for years, not knowing who to send it too then.

At first thinking it was ideal that I could work at a regular job and write as a hobby, to be able in that way not to have to worry about making my living writing.

But it was really my lack of ability to be a good writer, as well as realizing nobody wanted to hear about "Equality" at that time 50 years ago or even now, about what I myself was just beginning to know the what's and why's, that needed to be written about.

Religious leaders lead by encouraging and then enforcing their favorite customs and traditions of the past onto the sheep, to solidify and rally up emotions of belief for the present, with hopes of establishing their preferences for the future!

So again of course God was right. It was necessary for me to experience what God wanted me to write about, from the top to the bottom of the barrel.

To first have everything, a perfect time to be born in a perfect family, in a perfect democracy for a female of my time.

To be a successful Woman, then to lose everything, and to learn how to live again from scratch in poverty with nothing but a beautiful family and friends, which is everything, when you think about it. As long as you have enough to eat, sleep!

To learn the great and necessary value of safety nets, like the necessity for most here in America of having Car, House, Life insurance, if you have your own family and are the main breadwinner!

Reasons why we need seeming so much in a country, world, created for all, not just 1%, 2%, 10-20%, but for All so there are no cracks, as much as possible. Could be like heaven here on earth, as well as after this life. Both promised in scriptures to be possible eventually. When good people are willing to do what they can, with God's Help!

Satan has tried in many ways to do me in, starting at my birth with the cord so tightly wrapped around my neck I came out blue, if my father hadn't insisted on having a Doctor deliver me at home, not usual in those days. My life would have just ended then. He had to spend most of his last month pay, with a worker's strike and no welfare or unemployment insurance in those days, most felt lucky just to have a job, in those middle 1930's here in America, right after a depression.

Unions were needed to achieve the good wages, to be a voice for safe working conditions, benefits during a needed strike.

Even today those going out on a known legal union strike are still often denied unemployment benefits in many places. One thing besides many other political things that have really hurt the workers or the people's unions. One of the few helper's workers do have just for them!

Yes, you do have to watch out for signs of corruption, that is true in any organization you belong to. Have to be aware and as involved as you can be.

That is also true in any endeavor of your life, there are always going to be people who occasionally will see it in their best interest to take advantage of you and will justify it if you don't complain or notice, justifying maybe you don't care enough or it happened to them!

Freedom from oppression and slavery in the workplace or home is better now because others have paid such a great price for it, somewhere in the past, so don't just take it for granted.
To the extent it is yours you need to make sure it is not lost again and is protected for the next generation, it will be at least partly your responsibility to see that it stays.

Legal regulations are needed in all areas of politics and for economic policies, anywhere money and power are involved. Two of the greatest physical temptations for most people are yes, money and power over others, in those who are weak spiritually!
Needed work regulations and legal protections should be in place and monitored by unions, to keep workers and the management as honest as possible.

My Dad decided in good conscience not to go back to work in the tire factory, knowing he would refuse to walk across the picket line. They had decided to strike just about the same time I was born. His factory became one of the first of the workers in the US to form Unions, for what they knew should be for better wages, better working conditions, as well as many other such critical matters needed for the workers safety.

The managers and owners finally did begin to give some needed concessions of safety after much talk, after not thinking the workers would dare risk losing their jobs, their very lives, but many did.
Today many seem to have forgotten or never have been taught how much the workers gained from Unions of workers acting together for the benefit of all, at that time or not realized the benefits or rights of people's unions.

A physical as well as a spiritual trial for my Dad because he very much liked his job, by being able to make what to him was very good money, compared to farming but he knew with God's help, to choose what would be the best for all, and could not, would not, cross the workers picket line.

Yet we were some of the more fortunately ones who did have a family to go back to, who would take him and his new family in, another Cross for them, as well as the loss of a good job in times such as those.
They had to go back to the hardness of the farmers life that he had already known, especially in the hard times of those days.
So true of many decisions we must make in our lives without knowing at the time all of what the outcomes will be, only in having the faith that God is good and will eventually work it out for our better good and if not possible for us, at least for others in the long run, when we choose to do what we believe is the righteous thing to do.
Much less stressful if you have experienced God for yourself and know how to confirm with God's Holy Spirit about the universal Golden Rule.

Pro-Life, and Pro-Choice political decisions in voting now both seem equally true. It is when we get into others primarily males, being able to force a lifetime of being a Mother on what in most cases is just a child herself, that does not seem very equitable.

Praying now for a reconciliation between the two, being both moral-legal decisions. Human Rights for the unborn as well as for those already born! Should start first for the mother not last, be in favor for the already born when a choice has to be made! Her body and life being equally as precious, whether pregnant from rape, incest, her own sexual hormonal lack of control, or a lack of contraception!

Forced now to be responsible for the physical, mental, spiritual growth of herself as well as another child, to the degree all are affected. In studies, over 70% of criminals in prison have admited to have been mistreated, abused, unloved from being raised in such homes where they were unwanted. So, for most unborn by forcing their birth, may not be doing them any favor and God by nature allows over 15-20% of all pregnancies to miscarry in the first 6 weeks.

Only way for all to be Free is by keeping the female, as well as the male with the rights to their own bodies to be able to have our own Life, Liberty, and Pursuit of Happiness. Except in marriage where both have vowed to belong to each other, to become One in mind and heart.

Unborn rights, legally extending not beyond the danger to the Mother's life should consider her need to care for other children, or even those starving by the 1000's daily for lack of food, care, should have as much right to life, those already born!

To the extent the unborn are humanly developed enough to feel pain about four to five months and can live outside the Womb to be taken and given to another, puts the final decision in the hands of a Doctor and Surgeon, sworn to deal with the moral-legal decisions. With the financial burden primarily provided by the Family involved where possible, if not, by the Community, County, or State.

Based on moral-legal premises, all human life has the right to be cared lovingly in family settings, until able to provide financially for self.

We each need to stop, take time to ask what right we have to make choices of what is within the body of another.

WHAT ELSE CAN BE DONE?

It would be twenty-five more years after my seeing God's Hand as a Child, before being given the Word of "Equality", during my spiritual 'Rebirth'. The 'rebirth' Jesus taught we all need to have.

Would later read over 200 times in Biblical Scriptures, where God's Hand has been seen but mostly felt, in acting in doing God's Will rather than just self-interest.

During the time of Moses and many centuries later, in Daniels time, after his nation had been conquered by Babylon. While a King and his guests where feasting on Sacred vessels, taken from the destroyed Temple in Jerusalem, on their banquet wall God's Hand could be seen writing a message only Daniel was later able to interpret.

The Israelites had been conquered because of their sin of turning away from Godly ways, to bring them back to, to rid them of sinful leaders who mislead them with lies and self- interest, instead of all the peoples prosperity.

I was shown God's Hand only a month after Hitler, on the other side of the World was elected President of Germany. More than anyone else, responsible for more deaths than anyone during World War II, over 30 million. In our thousands of years of history, his hate and beliefs of inequality were responsible more!

Now, years later for last couple years, feeling the same dread felt during that World-Wide Disaster, another WWIII or now seeing this Biblical kind of Viral Plague, God has allowed to help us prevent a WWIII? We could still have both, it may depends of how soon this virus rebalances our lives to live more the Golden Rule by putting into practice the treating of others, all others, as you would want to be treated, with equal fairness, with "Equality".

Raised in a Christian Family from my Mother's Womb we were often in a Church called the "First Christian Church".
The teachings of the New Covenant after Jesus gave His human life, as a sacrifice for repented human sins!
Crucified on a cross three days later resurrected, "by his stripes we are healed" Is. 53:5 Seen by many over 40 days, before assuming into Heaven. Telling his followers to wait before they acted to receive God's Holy Spirit, at Pentecost. Acts Chapter 2. That would give them Godly power.

To "Love One Another", "Even your Enemies". Found in Matthew 5:44; 7:12; 22:39; Luke 6:27. Love ourselves, love the good life enough to want to be Spiritual Reborn.

Then find ways to stop sins of economic inequalities. The forces now in control of this physical world are not weak, maybe never have ever been stronger, but then so are God's people! Choosing God's Holy Spirit to guide will give you supernatural power and knowledge.

St. John had three visions, later combined in the last book of the Bible. He was the last of the original twelve followers of Jesus. Revelations talks about the evils of the end times, was given to warn of the consequences of not choosing to live in peace with one another!

The last Prophecy in Revelations 20 tells of a possible '1000 years' of Peace and could be instead of more war and as one of our human free will choices, if we change our ways of inequality. We could have that "1000 years of peace" if people were really willing to turn from the evils or booty of war. Not possible anymore if we allow inequality to continue to rule!

There are people, some we know in positions of power, who do not really have feelings for others, except possibly those close to them they believe are loyal to them.
Their feelings so selfishly held anyone who is not loyal or of value to them, they find hard to have any real feelings. They may be very good at pretending to be interested until you no longer serve their purpose or perceived as no longer loyal then are capable of striking like a snake, for evil lives within them.

Even see the value of rights but not interested in protecting other's rights, not directly valuable to them. Best they not be in any positions of power, believers in inequality!

Among the nations of today, many are trying to exert their control in the world, we here in America are one among them. Most of us want our Country to have high standards, yet we import food and products supporting those in control of countries known to use slave or very low wage laborers, who oppress the people! Do not support such inequality.

Jesus came not for the self-righteous, but to help us be honest with ourselves! If we won't be honest with ourselves, we won't be with others.

For now, Fr. Roy Bourgeois continues to serve some of the poorest of the poor, without the benefits retired Priest enjoy, after almost 50 years of giving all to The Church.

Recently his work has been used to bring attention to Georgia's Fort Benning, the military training school, after learning South American Dictators have been sending their military for training here. For their 'mob' control.

To continue the wage slavery of the people. Done so we, here in the U.S., can continue to benefit materially from forced low wages in most South American countries. To suppress people's rights and freedoms we in North America claim to cherish so much... at least for ourselves!

Another wrong that shouldn't be, paid for by the people's tax dollars. Let him know you support his work at his SOA Watch, PO Box3330, Columbus, GA. 31903.

Within the world's largest Catholic Communities of Priest, Sisters, Religious and laity, many have left, unable to accept the discrimination of the female half. Many more have left because of the many years of overlooked sexual abuse!

Pope Francis seems to be the first Pope to at least want to try to stop the travesty of the sexual abuse of children, insisting to first report it to your local police. He is concentrating on bringing in youth to join and should be but without equal rights for the female half?

Please pray the Church will recognize the Ministerial Gifts of Godly women who feel God's call of Priestly Vocations!

We need many notes to Pope Francis Apostolic Palace, Rome, Italy. 00120. Help your own religious groups to end discrimination or inequality that you know of.

Could determine our own Blessings Within, as well as Without. In our day, how many petitions, letters, or some form of protest would it take, to accomplish not only a worldwide minimum wage, but a needed cap on charging Interest, profits, to help decrease the inequality?

Excess profits beyond reasonable administrative cost could be used to provide a more equitable sharing of profits for all the workers labor efforts, and their time, life's energy.

Most people as One big block make up our biggest union, needing to work together for a fair shake in our world's economy, as a Democratic People's Right, not to mention a God given Right! God will Bless non-violent efforts!

Desperately needed to save lives and the quality of life of basic safety nets for children Worldwide, may need to be done working with International groups like the United Nations who work with the poorest to have a chance to learn to read or write, develop a skill according to their abilities, not just forced into the work place in slave like wages, as early as 5-7 years old. www. doctorsbeyondborders.org is also a good International organization that works with the poorest.

When you ask God to help you! We must think of others, as well as ourselves, for moral, mental, emotional well-being. See all, as your neighbors no matter where they live! Don't doubt God's non-partial Love for all!

There are many legal, non-violent ways, when people realize, see the needs. Find others to work with, in everyone's long-term best interest. Work we will always need for substance, and health, a Vocation also equally needed for our Spirit. Souls.

Are not the worlds resources, the source of providing the profits through people's labor, here for the benefit of all and not just for excessive profits of a few?

Our worlds previous customs and traditions of inequality, such as female bondage, slavery, racism as well as unfair wages came originally from the waring and conquering by males, thousands of years ago established a belief of inequality and 'might makes right' by both physical force and misuse of weapons.

Later males in control used the written word to support control speaking as god's through male/only religions. Yet we were created Co-Creators in God's Image. Created to be equal helpers to each other. Not to be gods over others, but to care and serve one another.

Saw a sign in a Church yard on a bus this morning that said, "No time to throw stones, when washing someone's feet".

Jesus taught us to serve each other, did by example much more of His teaching than has been recorded.

Our world needs an equal balance and tolerance for others in our religious, political, and economic systems.

Such as what is commonly found in Hospital work. First the observant Intake workers, in the Nurses, Doctors, first to observe, listen, rightly evaluate each situation, they have learned to act with a Cool Head and without Partiality, to decide the priority of the sickness, or need. All are treated equally each patient in the proper order for each.

I feel a need to warn you, our world is more like a battle field, badly needing a medical staff, it really is going to be up to you those reachable now, willing to confirm in their own hearts the rightness and need to have your own "Rebirth" experience with God's Holy Spirit, able to hear and follow Godly guidance you are going to need, for mental, emotional, spiritual, as well as physical survival as this Biblical viral plague like many before, brings out the best as well as the worse in us.

Most of us are born, ready and capable of loving others, as well as ourselves, unless or until, we suffer too much hurt or damage, then we tend to block such feelings in a natural survival instinct, or in the dread of experiencing more hurt!

Such damage to, any negative indoctrination in your early childhood may not even be remember in the conscious mind.

If severe enough closed off into an unconscious mind or memory, to come out later in hard to understand kinds of reasonings, resentments, fears, even hate, when you again feel similarly threatened!

In some, rarely, for others may never be able to develop normally. True for many Dictator types seeking power for inner needs to control others. Becoming natural to strongly seek positions of power, justify the use of inequality, as a needed means of controlling others. They will feel no reason to change.

Here in 2020 have many in high places, yet less than in past times! We must continue to improve as dictators are dangerous for all on our planet.

I Pray more and more good people will seek more interest in politics and religion, by seeing the need for good and loving hearts in leaders.

Those who want to control others to satisfy something missing within their development tend to use efforts to care as a means to deepen their control, only feeling secure in loving themselves, those they see as being like themselves as long as they know they have their loyalty.

So difficult for such a person to experience God's Holy Spirit of Love. So, for your own safety it is best just to pray for, avoid if possible and put in God's Hands.

When in doubt discern as soon as possible, for your own possible role or safety. Crimes of such madness and passion are some of the most common. Be cautious when you notice any sign. The Holy Spirit of God is your only known for certain guide I've known.

All of us have and need ways from past fears and hurts that tends to be self-centered, within our needy human physical natures, making it hard to see, to realize our being spiritual as well as a physical part of the wholeness of our nature.

In hearts and minds that have not been too hurt or too damaged, we expect and want to be equally or fairly treated, as well as feel a need to treat others with an equal fairness. For those who can, it will mean being able to feel sorrow, when you realize you have hurt others, then look for those who have hurt you and forgive, as you are forgiven only to the extent that you are able to forgive others!

To really want to seek a new beginning, to experience for yourself this Holy Spirit kind of Love, get to know the best possible kind, nothing less, not likely without God's Help.

For most of us each inch of the way in forgiving, you should feel padded on the back, it is hard for our ego but good later increasing Godly courage and strength, that starts with sincerely asking for such help and trusting that it will invariably come, for then God will help you make the best of it sooner or later.

Even if having to be a Martyr puts you in Sainthood, you don't want to try out for less in this life! Few of us will even come close. So at least head for the best!

When asking God to be forgiven, don't doubt you will be if sincere, you should be able to experience, feel the forgiven Peace. If you don't, think over if maybe it is you, who have not been able to forgive certain others, you may still need to forgive, even of your own forgiveness?

You may need more spiritual guidance, than I can give you. If in doubt, seek someone you have reason to believe knows a Loving God.

Be sure to first pray and ask in faith to be led to the right person for you. Just by being willing to open up to spiritual hearing, you are more likely to find that person.

Easier to feel harmony, not only in your own being but with others when we are willing to let go of negative feelings, especially those damaging ones of unforgiveness, they hurt us more than they hurt anyone else and why it is important to seek, find, and get rid of any negative feelings, consciously and unconsciously, as professional help is usually needed for uncovering built up over time unconscious negative feelings.

I needed three years of help, an hour a week, to release those of mine, Thankfully, by good Catholic Christian Doctors, Plus a weekly group of eight other Patients, an hour of taking turns being on a hot seat of each examining our motives, guilt, fears and dislike of our lives up to that point.

Another abused ex-wife, my own self-pity feelings I was never going to get physically well again and unable to accept being at the bottom of my health and needs. I had stopped wanting to live. In my lack of understanding God's Will of my need to experience real poverty, not just my chosen voluntary one and then climb out of my "self-pity" took me three years, but I now cherish those humbling years and many times over Thank God for experiencing them, what I learned, in no other way! After the traumas of an accident at work, leaving me unable to do the work I loved but was adding to the rich style of life my vow of poverty would no longer allow!

Together I shared with another burned out Nurse, and a then depressed policeman who couldn't get rid of his once excessive violence that had killed (he admitted to only one) for a minor offense. There was a Priest too who had a vision of the Church turning upside down after Vatican II and because he thought Visions were something people had in Biblical days. He suspected someone playing a joke might have put acid in his coffee and so did his Bishop.

A Psychiatrist after a month of confinement in the hospital, three shock treatments, pills, plus the forever loss of his Parish, left him still in shock-like shakes needing much love and sympathy, I tried to help as he helped me to want to try to live again. He eventually was forced to retire.

Those who have not had to suffer that much hurt, have many times been miraculously released from their spiritual pain by just asking God for a new heart, for a spiritual "rebirth".

In the act of asking, a new beginning at least begins, an opening to the Holy, give thanksgiving for each new day able to have Holy Spirit's guidance in your heart confirmed, when doing God's Will!

Some of us will still have to each day forgive a little more, more fully releasing ourselves, for a Spiritual knowing of Blessings Within.

Avoid selfish, envious marks like those of the Curse of Cain: "Am I my brother's keeper"? In lacking an equal concern for others. Realizing many of world's children, not even allowed to go to school to learn to read and write, let alone develop talents, forced young to go to work for their daily food. This cannot be right?

Why should most people's labor, the world's resources, so needed for the benefit of all be hoarded by just a few? Best we work where and when we can, especially towards a world-wide living wage for all.

One way the US came out of the great 1929 depression was able bodied men were hired by the government to do work on roads and building great dams for electricity. They worked in forest, fire prevention jobs. Disability government payments for those unable to work, for each in America to at least have a living income. Now it can take up to 3 years for disability court hearing to see if one is eligible.

After being Spiritually "Reborn", our hearts are best kept open to possible ways we might be needed for our world to become a better place. God's Loving Presence living within our hearts, will urge us to a best possible response. Not always at the time apparent, it may mean the patience to wait, listen, look, to see!

An answer will come when you seek the better ways! When you are weak or weary, seemingly without a friend, rest in the pillows of God's understanding and compassion, always right beside you and more reliable than any other.

Most of us won't bother to turn to, except when in Dire Need, what should be our first turn to. God's Spirit as best advisor. We tend to prefer what is seen, like a visible human or an animal companion.

Try to get in the habit of spending at least one minute, work up to five most days then you can make a habit of spending at least 10-15 min. alone with God. The only God worth your worship!

No way can I tell you how much you will be rewarded, after a while you will realize these are the most important peaceful minutes of your day!

Our unconditional Loving and Knowing God already knows, all things about us so we never need to disguise or deny or hide any human weakness and who holds all of our needs.

When we do seek help, advice, or just need to resist what is tempting, distracting us from better purposes, we will be richly rewarded and soon realize a greater way than any of our own possibilities!

Down through human history, people living together in community have agreed on, or had leaders forced on them, who ruled over then. There are dangers in allowing other people instead of God's Holy Spirit, to govern.

God warned the Hebrews in the Bible, having just Judges were all they needed. Yet they insisted on having their own Kings like the rest of the world had. The Prophet Samuel warned them, it would not be good for them, and it sure hasn't been, or for most other nations as well.

The first chosen people like the rest of us, failed God, time after time. All of us even the smartest, wisest, need daily contact and friendship with The Creator of All, for each one's Benefit. Even Eternal Life is only a Promise for those willing to keep on Trusting who follow the Creator of all!

So easy for human Kings, Rulers of all kinds, to become like Dictators, or to think they are Superior with the right to take the best from the people and offer little in exchange. Power becomes like any form of evil, addictive.

Such power comes in other ways too, by selling, loaning, and buying with Usury or Interest, high profits on Loaning, profits above a reasonable business or administrative cost, and why it is to be avoided, not even allowed in many religions. Forbidden in most Scriptures money gained just for a profit, or as unrighteous profits on the profits.

Have heard recently all kinds of bad mouth talk raising fears and concerns about the UN. Can't help but wonder how much of it is meant to discredit, in particular the rights of females and other individual people's rights. As if more of human rights are worse.

Besides the danger of world Dictators which we already have or whoever has the biggest and most bombs, since the rise of fascism in Hitler's time, in WWII, we have needed a United Nations Organization since then, with the little-known human rights laws in their Charter needing now to be much better known.

Established in 1945, to encourage respect for human rights, to prevent ever again the fascist destruction of human rights as happened in World War II.

"Whereas the people of the United Nations have in this Charter reaffirmed their faith in fundamental human rights, the dignity and worth of the human person, and the equal rights of men and women…Now, therefore the General Assembly proclaims this Universal Declaration of Human Rights as a common standard of achievement for all peoples and all nations…" *

*Preamble of Universal Declaration of Human Rights in 1948. Much like our own Declaration of Independence.

The advantages of people and nations working together for a better and freer world, especially from war and injustice, needs our American support. To continue to do all the good work they have and are doing, to be adopted by many nations to prevent corruption by the people freely being able to elect representatives.

Human rights include not only the right to life, liberty, but a freedom from oppression, from wage slavery, not to mention torture, or not having enough to eat, for basic living needs.

The right to have an education, as far as one has the ability and the desire to learn, maybe being the best way to keep our human rights from ever again taken away.

As long as so many of our world's children, estimated at over half, are not allowed free and available education to have a chance at a chosen and decent job in our world, we will continue to have people taking advantage of them as we remain at risk under the 1% controlling our economy.

Until we are willing to work with others, by using the United Nations International rules of law to find support, such as the American ACLU previous mountains of legal work. The peoples Freedom, and Democracy tied more than ever to having only the very best of people representing people's needs and interest, having their voices heard, as well as assurance of each person's vote. To be fairly counted in elections, each one equally represented!

The Golden Rule as the best Rule, why I am strongly Pro-Life but equally Pro-Choice for each one's individual right of life within them.

Once a child is born it has all the same legal rights anybody else has but no one has the right to take the woman's right to freely choose to have a child. Such as the government in China controls caps on population with pills or abortion. Our Souls being Spiritual God can give or take, unknown to us when it is given. God Created the woman's body to reject over 10-15% with natural miscarriages during the first couple months and up to 5-10% after six weeks until Birth, often before the Mother even suspects, except maybe for an extra heavy period.

What possible right, does another person have to force a woman, at any time to a lifelong care/concern for a child?

As existed before contraceptives. Any of us may try to help an unwanted pregnancy, to offer free maternal care before and after birth. Adoption of the child into a loving home. Still the birth mother must be free to make the final decision to keep or give the child up.

Only the woman, hopefully with a Doctor and if there is a loving partner or husband to support her decision but she remains free, others or a government should not be able to make or force such a choice on anyone else's womb.

Studies have found at least 70% of those who end up in prisons, tell of knowing or feeling unwanted growing up, of being abused physically, mentally, emotionally, or sexually, by one or more messed up, immature or just not parent material who were forced into parenthood or not wanting a child, at least not at that time, then are seldom able to bond, as a parent must, to raise a mentally healthy or loving child.

At this time, I would support laws for a legal terminating of an unwanted pregnancy during the last one/third semester to save an unborn if determined by two Doctors for variable survival and adoptive care for the child is available.

A birth of unwanted child should be put into the care of another stable reliable Parent or adoptive parent if at all possible, or as a ward of the state, until the Mother or relative or an adoptive, can be shown to be willing to be a caring parent/guardian of the child.

With all these dangers we now face, a time to being open to a Loving God of Equality for all. You will have to Confirm for yourself, knowing all of us will feel pulled towards the influence we have had the most of in our past. Try to commit today to confirm first with God.

For so many young people and from the experience in my own youth many begin to doubt at least after tragedy's, traumas, when we expect a good God to protect us and when not, become disillusioned of a childlike faith.

This kind of thinking blocked my once good relationship I had with God, and in my hurt was not able to realize our free will choices, the decisions we make.

God does not ever take away from our free will, for this is what keeps us from having just a wild animal nature, or be unfeeling robots but nature as well as other people exercising their free will allows bad things to happen to good people, just as good things happen to some very bad people.

Until we spiritual mature we cannot possibly know all of many of the reasons why, we have to grow in faith, of a loving God who does know so much more of the past, present and future than we do. Yet still honors our free will choices! With a great consolation that God can and does eventually bring good out of the worse that can happen, at least for those who are willing to continue to love both God and each other. We have to trust in unseen faith, in a greater wisdom to follow, the value of a Holy Love for one another, the basis of the best Spiritual laws, and how we are eventually going to have to learn to use our free will to live together in peace to be found worthy of eternal life.

It can be a tempting path sometimes, when highways of high living can seem to be more fun, easy to fall into traps that look harmless. I Praise God for helping me to get free when I could have been caught, maybe permanently?

Most of us experience, sooner or later injustices we want to blame others or our Creator, when we are living in a world with many gods of inequality and ignorance in high places!

Do not lose faith in a Loving God's Help to bear whatever you encounter, try to think of it as a time of testing and of strengthening your Faith. God remains always right by your side just not willing to control us, but willing to help us grow to our perfection.

Keep a point of contact, by taking your first few moments of the day to say "Good Morning" "what can I best do today?" and at the end, return your thoughts in thanksgiving, to the God who is always there for comfort if you've willing to follow righteous ways!

Don't gaze at circumstances without spiritual eyes too, focus on finding the blessings within. Or you will tend to lose sight of your center, the One who never changes.

You will change in your perceptions, but remember to keep your spiritual mind above the fray, staying close to the source of constant flowing, alive, Spiritual Water. Drink as often as you need, seeking forgiveness for others, as well as yourself, when needed with a conscious desire to know and do what your best is.

Once you have had your spiritual "rebirth" then when you have a question or decision to make, you will know and feel free to talk directly to God, usually just in your mind best, in daily quiet times.

I had sensed, maybe told, at least somehow knew, after my baptism I should do that, but failed to make a habit of it, partly for having very little quiet time, in a small family home with four active children, busy parents and being very active myself, what seemed mostly to be in good ways, even working the last year of high school, after school, from 3 till 10pm. Working the legal max. of time where we lived, before the age of 18, in our little local Hospital, which gave me with only one registered Nurse on a shift, the chance to learn and help even in minor surgery, in the newborn Nursery, E.R, room, in those days nightly back rubs for each patient who could turn sideways, if not on their stomach.

Feeling very capable of thinking, doing, grown up at that age, maybe from the early death of my Father at 14, that made for an easy breaking of the parental umbilical cord having a sense of freedom and self-worth, a value to myself and others.

When you are willing to talk with God in your thoughts, you should usually get a response or answer, you learn to listen until you recognize a Godly thought, coming into your mind. There are many ways God chooses to respond to us, very rarely, at least for me by a spoken or heard Word, or just by thoughts in my head that are distinctly different, not being in my regular way of thinking.

Some may get whole sentences. Blessed are they, I may not be as holy, only God knows, so trying to compare anyone else to yourself as being better or worse, is a drain and a waste of what little but precious blessings, time and energy we each have.
Those who have more, still have more moral or social responsibility to do more, so it all tends to even out.

You may not even recognize a response to your prayers right away, but later by what you read or hear, the answer can have a way of standing out as specifically meant for you, when you do get your answer. It may also be a "No", that we usually do not want to hear, accept, and sometimes just don't.

Find comfort knowing in the long run a better 'Yes' for you, will be. God's Will is never selfish or self-centered like Ours tends to be.

Need also to be more willing to accept, trust in the Holy Spirit's guidance, once you have had a spiritual 'rebirth', for you then have The Christ Promise of eternal life too.

That kind of hope and faith will help you be able to spiritually see far more than you otherwise could in this short span of living. Adding more Blessings that bring both Peace and Joy! In spite of what is happening in the world all around!

Sometimes when you find doubts creeping in, the only way of knowing, seems to come when you ask and are given answers to your questions and realize you couldn't possibly have known that on your own. In experiencing this for yourself or learning from someone you trust of their particular miracles that had no known physical cause!

Remember miracles are rare and if they were commonly seen, we couldn't call them miracles. They are always way out of the ordinary kind of happenings. Yet as real as any other reality. Sometimes they are just not so well understood as a natural good happening. I think I've seen both kinds, and in both kinds there is a specialness to be thankful for!

I would not actually physically see anything, the second time of experiencing God's Hand very strongly, both times many years apart, and did feel and recognize the same strong presence of God, as at my spiritual rebirth. The feeling of The Holy Spirit as it came through the walls of my house, like an

Ocean Wave of Holy Loving Presence, washing over me, and the Supernatural Cleansing of everything in the room.

In ordinary times of deep prayer or when needing to talk, usually only feel a gentle, loving presence, like when you know your conscience is especially righteous with God, and you feel whole. A sense of being close to, and on Holy Ground.

Thank Goodness I was sitting down the first two times of experiencing an actual physically felt Spiritual presence.

In Biblical Scriptures even grown men have fallen face down, by the strong presence of experiencing a physical appearance, as well as the Spiritual nearness of God, that just in receptive moods we can more easily tune into. See Ezekiel 1:28; 2:2.

It troubled my mind in the weeks and months after I first heard the Word of "Equality", from what I had been taught about morality in a man's world, and this was in the early 60's. Days of hearing lots of fearful news in the US, mostly by Senators talking and debating. Remembering one of the Senators Joe McCarthy's emphasizing the dangers of Russia's Communism.

I finally began to realize how we were being propagandized in many way's and forms in all kinds of media, like in war movies, as well as in the general news against anything relating to Russia.

Due to the cold war, both governments were waging in those days, and still are. In each of their battles to see who has the biggest or the most! Also realize I repeat here but was reminded if it seems important to clarify alright to emphasize.

Not until I read the Gospels of Jesus with the word of "Equality" in mind, would I recall how Jesus and the early believers had lived a communal life, that continued for most Christians for the first 300 years after the Resurrection of Jesus, until Christianity became an official Roman Empire kind of religion.

Still the communal custom continued in most religious communities among religious members as a way of making sure each has what they need by mutual sharing, according to the needs of each, much as in the way most good families try to care for each other.

Russia's or china's practice of Communism is not considered good examples of communal living, both are corrupted and controlled from the top down, instead of the bottom up and not by law are people equally represented. True in most groups controlled or overseen as power can easily just become addictive for those seeking power and tends to be corruptive by it's open to dictatorship.

We need to reinforce a People's Democracy of each committed to putting into practice a Community Co-Op' run by the people for the benefit of the people, to meet the needs of the people.

Allowing profit-making enterprises for those things above and beyond necessities needed for life, essential foods, as well as for the normally needed services for fire, police services, health too, best run on a non-profit basis, by local elected Councils, with regional, even up to joining for International help, as needed.

A separate employee-controlled Union, representing all people's needs not just employee's!

Having sufficient legal safeguards to prevent unscrupulous or criminal behavior from taking over management, from the top down, and by elected judges or overseer's, locally to the Supreme Court, not politician appointees.

Even religious and non-profit institutions can become corrupt under the rule of 'might makes right', as in the rule of Gold, rather than The Golden Rule, written by God into loving hearts, as long as they have not been too damaged.

Believers continue good works as good people have always done, following a Holy Love and caring for one another, in the family and community.

After the darker ages of our history, like before the beginning of the Printing Press, the means of sharing communications, were now many people are able to read scriptures for themselves. Although women were still discouraged, from learning to read or write, until comparatively recent times in the late 19th-20th Century. In some places still lag.

In Christianity the contrast between the teachings of Jesus and the institutions of inequality, discrimination and other abuses of power, resulting in much loss of belief, in spiritual confusion. Creating as the same time many smaller Christian Protestant Groups.

While some set specific dogmas required for membership for believers, others became more Democratic. Most pleased to have you come if you felt comfortable with the Pastor's message.

Customs of discriminations and inequality are worldwide. Customs of political and economic beliefs of inequality, 'might makes right', are common when patriarchal religious male nouns and pronouns support the false idolatry of a male only controlling God.
Disastrously affecting relations between the sexes, political relationships between nations, as well as the economic systems and markets.

Most controlling economic males stay behind the scenes as much as possible, to be able to more safely manipulate the money systems. Using CEO's and managers out front to do their will, to increase profits. Also controlling lending organizations with higher Interest or Usury the charging of more than the reasonable cost for the use of money, for ever more profits!

Some of these little-known people of power, organizations and money-making businesses, built many years ago and passed down through intermarriage, family backing, and by an inheritance and knowledge of stocks and bonds and the Corporate world. Political influence, by largest contributors in their specific areas of political interest is part of the control.

After my own spiritual "rebirth" I did not feel at first led to join or Witness to the Catholic Church, having heard rumors since childhood. Did not even know of a Vatican II for over 10 years after this ever so often World Council of Bishops at Vatican II happened in 1965 and published in their Pastoral Constitution a significant statement as The Church of so over a million was "to end discriminations of both race and sex as not God's Will." But later failed to give equal rights for Ordination for the female half who had felt called by God.

Not that God didn't already know they were not going to act on it, but I've wondered if God was not willing to give Pope John Paul II and his close Vatican II companion who would later walk in his shoes as Benedict XVI, their own time to use, or misuse the throne of Peter. That of course is only for God to Judge.

None of us are capable of knowing all or what influences The Popes are under. When I want to put blame on any one of them, I am reminded of the dagger I saw close to the back of Pope John Paul II, in a vision of his hands tied behind his back, not long before he was finally bedridden.

Giving me renewed hope of eventually reaching our now Holy Pope Francis. This largest of all Christian groups with God's Word of "Equality".

Still looking to finding a way to appeal to both faith and reason. Gradually realizing many Catholic leaders and even more lay members had yet to even hear, or maybe just didn't want to hear at the time, The Holy Spirit's message to The Church to end discrimination for the female half too.

By the 1980's Pastors and Bishops began to have weekend trainings in The Church for much-needed volunteer laity of either sex to become what was then called extra-ordinary Ministers, female as well as male altar-servers!
A seemingly first step towards ending discrimination, and towards Ordination, but in actuality has just been a token step, for The Church has really needed the extra distributors of Communion, from the loss of Priest leaving and increasingly the number of Catholics now being able to take full Communion.

As Equals No. As Equal Sharers on the Altar No. As equal workers yes, they at least have been accepted as that so long as the women kept their place as laity and did not aspire to be Ordained!
They are a real help to the Priest, and the Congregation, in those and many other ways, such as visiting the sick, even possible with the Sacraments now, that have already been consecrated.

A Loving and Highly Discerning Monk, not long after my first retreat from hearing about the now rights of women to be Altar Servers within The Church, rightly helped bring me down to face reality again, from my original excitement, of being able to actually be one of these first "Extra-Ordinary" Ministers.

By telling me, they were soon going to be a "dime a dozen" and I should concentrate on what the Lord wanted me to do. I had not spoken about anything like that to him and he had never met me before or since, but of course he had the gift of discernment and I'm sure The Lord inspired him to tell me.

Still I loved being one of the first Extra-Ordinary Ministers and had to force myself to stop, when God started urging me to find a way to get to Rome.

Then I would hear of a hundred Catholic women, who had also felt God's call, and who had already gone successfully through the Catholic Theological Training needed to serve as Priests, who became the first examples of really ending sexism in The Church.

Actually Ordained, by legal Catholic Bishops, as only Bishops in The Church can do the Ordaining. These first hundred ordained Women Priest are still being rejected by the Vatican, so they serve us now in the "Future Church". www.CatholicWomenPreach.org Catholic Women for Equality, www.WomenOrdination.org or www.futurechurch.org.

Help me pray God will give us more time, for this next generation seems so much more open! Yet this feeling of how close we are to war, that does not go away, nor do I see the best way to continue to appeal, except by continuing to try and reach those who will do what they can. Those who see the need.

Have learned not to run or avoid or escape from life's problems for when God directs, one's problems can become blessings, even actually designed for your growth, those seeking to be in God's Hand.
When the way before you appeares blocked focus on Jesus as your shepherd leading you along your life-journey. Before you know it the "obstacle" will be behind you and you will hardly know how you passed through it.

That is the secret of success. Although you remain aware of the visible world around you, your primary awareness is Me, you can trust to get you through rough patches with confidence, for God does what is right and smooths out the path ahead!

You can expect, by placing your faith in your Holy Spirit guidance, for good to eventually come, to find more ways or opportunities to help as well as increases your trust in a loving Heavenly Parent!

For when we don't understand enough, or feel confused, our certainty can be elusive, we may most need to increase our Faith in God's Perfect Being and Goodness.

Needs can then become doorways to a deeper reliance, to create a deeper dependency with the source of all Goodness.

Our naturally more imperfect self-reliance we need to give up, increase the dependency on the more Loving God, to show the way.

Allow such faith to grow, and it continues to grow as you allow. Remember there is no fooling God, like you can fool others. Your faith will tend to die when not relied on, trusted in!

In reading Scriptures if you are not realizing you are reading from God's human wholeness, from the words of only the male half, influenced by the Culture of that time that also justified all slavery, as well as female bondage, you may tend to misinterpret God's message that is coming through! Why you need The Holy Spirit and a spiritual "Rebirth", to Confirm for yourself! For the fullness of Truth!

Until around the 1500's AD Biblical Scriptures had been written by the Christian Priestly scribes on Scrolls in Hebrew, and Greek, along with the Aramaic teachings of Jesus like "ABBA" the Aramaic Word Jesus used for God, meaning "Heavenly Parent".

Only later when translated into Patriarchal (male) versions in different languages of English, Latin, Spanish, etc. "Abba" was translated only as "Father" yet theologically still included the Mother, but not clarified except among scholars. The meaning of "Father" when applied to God, includes the Mother too! Ask a scholarly Theologian.

So, it is easy to see why most people from childhood would fall into the idolatry of worshipping only a male image of God, including many Priest.

The culture deeply ingrained, of the female created to serve the male and the nurse maid remaining in second place status both culturally and legally, until the right of women to vote was finally won for women in America, in 1921. Nineteen hundred and twenty-one years after Jesus time here on earth!

Jesus probably came at the historical height of Slavery and Sexism, discrimination and inequality for most males as well as women. The Jewish Covenant or the first part of The Bible had already been completed in the Hebrew language many years before the time of Christ, and being seen as fulfilled by Christians in Jesus, as the awaited Messiah, or Christian Covenant the New testament. Together they make up the whole Bible, both the Hebrew Covenant and The New Covenant for all people, as understood by male Christians.

Since that first called Council by the Emperor of Rome to write The Bible, Catholic Councils have also been called within The Church, about every so many 100's of years.

The Vatican I Council during the 1800's and the last time in 1965, at Vatican II. Each time to make needed changes within the Canon law of The Church. Canon law as the interpreter of Scriptures and Living Scriptures within The Church that includes Vatican II's Pastoral Constitution to end Church discrimination for the female half of God's Image.

While the separated Christian Protestant Churches have for the most part been reluctant to add Catholic changes since the 1500's excommunication of Luther. A scholar and Monk, his attempt to return The Church to the example of the original followers of Jesus as was during the first 300 years, before The Church became a part of the political arm of the then Roman Empire.

Early Christians, by their teaching and spiritual gifts, mostly by word of mouth, had in spite of the dangers involved, appealed to primarily the poorest, the most oppressed. Especially women and slaves, who were trying to follow the example and teachings of Jesus as closely as possible.

Passed on the beliefs of Christian equal fellowship and often communal living, being as St. Paul in his Spiritual maturity put it as no Jew or Gentile, slave or free, rich or poor, male or female, but all One "In Christ". Galatians 3:28.

As some still do today, remain by choice the poor, even those who had the most to win, accepting this way of being able to see themselves and each other as spiritual equals.

By their example to witnessing and withstanding the persecution, they were able to keep the Church at that time very much alive and growing by following the teaching and example of Jesus.

What was maybe the most unusual and the most appealing to new converts at the time, was the love they showed each other by treating each with equal respect and equal concern to help each other feel equally loved by God, seeking to also follow Jesus example, in sharing according to the needs of the others.

Unlike the male dominating cultures of those times, and still in many of ours. Within the Christian communities the women served along with their male brothers, as they felt God had called them, with Spiritual gifts as Priests, Prophets, and Bishops, and all of the other Holy Spirit spiritual gifts such as Healers, Teachers, Helpers of all kinds.

Most of all to equally 'Love One Another', 'even their enemies', as Jesus had taught.

But in the later Roman culture of sexual inequality, males took over the official political Roman Catholic Church, excluding the female half and even most males, until recently by a communion rail from being able to come close to the communal altar.

Not until after the 1965 Vatican II Council, have they been willing to give their needed but only in token concessions for females, as well as male laity altar servers.

Even through the Holy Spirit spoke to the Bishops at Vatican II specifically saying in article 29 of their Pastoral Constitution "to end discrimination in The Church", yet the inequality for the female continues.

Will the female half be given in my great grandchildren's lifetime the opportunity for equal rights?

Believers who have had the experience of being "reborn" especially married couples know when they are not in agreement with one another, they can then go for guidance, along or together, to God's Holy Spirit. As a way for Peace Within, as well as Without.
A personal relationship with God's Holy Spirit is possible for those with clean hearts, willing to commit to living what Jesus taught!

Not only is a personal relationship possible, but a new heart can be given when you sincerely receive being spiritual "reborn". Then freed from inherited sin by the Grace of God through Jesus as Christ the awaited Messiah. The pure and holy sacrifice for humans, curing all infected with the curse of sin, those willing to receive it for the eternal spiritual life, we were originally created to have.

Giving a peace of mind, joy at times when bearing even painful trials while feeling God's Love and Presence. There is no other God to compare with, only worldly idol gods not worthy to worship!

We make the best use of our freewill, in cooperative freedom found in the Equal Rights of all. Rights that stop only at the rights of another!

THE EQUALITARIAN AGE

More than ever, we all need a Peaceful settlement, satisfactory to all sides to be able to prevent further retribution and hostility. The time as well as the need is here.

As we begin to send our rockets out into space, we also need to be concerned about whether there is life out there that is a threat to our planet if they feel threatened by us!

So much talk of UFO's, I've heard from truth telling people of their personal experiences. One of a small female Alien who before entering a small round craft, made a sign to my friend with her arms crossed in front of her, he told me only after he was diagnosed with a terminal cancer, that it had long puzzled him what it meant. I knew it as a Catholic sign of those who go before Priest in the line of Communion who wish to be Blessed by The Priest when they fold their arms in front of them!

My friend said this had happened as a young man, but he had hesitated to tell anyone about it, out of fear of being laughed at or they think he just had imaged it. He was not Catholic and would not have known of that sign I don't think. But it is a logical sign of someone who knew it as a sign of goodwill.

Have heard from a few others of seeing alien space craft, in the sky and have seen many credible stories on the History Channel but never had heard before of a female being seen. Know there are billions of other planets around millions of life-giving Suns. No one knows how many could have life similar to ours, would have to be further advanced.

The age of just our known universe is calculated over 2 billion years old at a minimum. It is possible for more advanced livable planets who have learned to live in peace and are in space exploration just as we have already started to be.

We also have scientific evidence now of our planet being bombarded daily with bacteria, and virus matter, both dead and alive that can live inside small, even molecular space debris, that gives evidence of life being possible beyond our planet. Incoming different kinds of virus probably are the cause of sudden outbreaks of deadly plagues all down through our history!

So, lots of potentials to ponder, but with very little provable conclusions, officially or publicly declared, that we can say beyond any doubt, at this point, about much life in the cosmos.

Yet anyone who has ever seen a clear night's view of the endless uncountable numbers of stars, known to be similar to our sun, with a number of planets going in circles around, known because they cast a shadow as they circle around, so we can hardly help but wonder about the endless possibilities and many now find it hard to believe there could not be unknown numerous kinds of living beings out there just in our observable universe from the space stations!

This is another important reason for people on our planet to stop fighting each other, to start working together in Peace and Goodwill. Since we are not able at this time to be certain about what motives, any potential for life out there might have in mind for us? Are they just looking, on vacation or in need? We have no way to know at this point.

Nor can life be limited to just what can be seen within our physical matter based just on our particular kind of carbon atoms.

We best not limit! From our known evidence of hard to know things: like electricity, energy, gravity, all the hidden life forms I have seen under a microscopic, in searching for our known diseases. X-rays, gamma rays, we know of only a small range beyond our limited physical matter. We do know there is potential for life everywhere, both friendly and not so friendly, we really do need to work together as a human family and not against each other in any negative way! Help us God to go towards the Best we can be at this time in our History. Trust, that most people will, as they realize more, extend their hand in concern for one another's mutual protection.

Many evidences within us of what we call extra ordinary Spiritual experiences, but usually not physically repeated on demand as required in for scientific studies.

When one has a personal encounter with what they believe is spiritual, it can best be judged by whether it is harmful or helpful to that person or to the whole for the common good.

A Spiritual encounter from a Loving "Heavenly Parent" of All, would be primarily for the common good of All!

Negative encounters from a negative spiritual source would be for more selfish purposes to frighten, control or even gain entrance to a body or soul, by taking over ones free will?

Better off avoiding as many negative encounters as possible.

While understanding that people who have never experienced any kind of a spiritual encounter may be naturally doubtful or fearful even in knowing about such Spiritual beings.

Some are sincere in asking for a sign, a natural need for some of miraculous sign of certainty, and when not receiving one can easily conclude there is no such being, failing to understand other factors like sin, or lack of faith and belief could affect being able to spiritually "see or hear"!

That happened to me in in my late teens just because I felt so deserted and betrayed by what I had assumed was my agreement with God to be able to have a family instead of being a nun. After I had chosen a young man and at his death, before we married, had not realized or been warned any choice we make in our free will choices, there will be the potential for troubles and when there is grief, often anger and resentment I felt that we had not at least been warned.

Now I understand that even in trusting in God's eventual better way would not have necessarily meant an easy way. In my grief I felt no response to my questions. No help I felt I needed at that time, and because I was probably so upset I couldn't 'hear' so concluded what I thought had been a good relationship with God was maybe just in my mind's imagination.

Even began to wonder if God was dead or not real as many seemed to believe, or in another part of the universe. Complete uncertainty for the first time in my life…

It would be nine years before I would not just ask for a sign from God but be willing to ask again in faith, by first repenting of all or any of my wrong thinking, actions, by doing a deep spiritual cleaning, before I would finally receive an answer.

Finally after a kind of fleece, a first step-in-faith needed to have a response, but more than a 100-fold rewarded as all such quests are eventually answered, as I can now 'see'!

We do not have either God's knowledge or control over what is best for us to know at any specific time and in trying to insist to know why things happen or to try to conjure up a Spirit for answers is asking for trouble, or only silence at best!

Better to seek spiritual things with the "faith of a mustard seed" and the patience it will take. It took me two weeks of constantly keeping a prayer on my lips, even fasting for a sign, with just enough food as I still had to work but fasting in other things. Most of all accepting God's best timing, if there was at that time in my thinking, a real intelligent Creator a Loving God.

Signs are rarely given on demand. From what I've learned, only in specific circumstances are any miraculous signs given at all. Sooner or later most of us will learn or experience for ourselves that "the rain as well as the sun falls on the good as well as the bad", for God is "not a god of partiality". *

*Duet.10:18; Act:10:34; Romans 2:11

Many of us tend to lose faith like I did, when bad things happen to seemingly good people, seemingly so unfairly.

Natural to feel if there had been a Good God in charge, we each would be equally protected from harm.

I have known that feeling well. Have been so very fortunate to have known what it is like to have miraculous things happen, but never just for a special favor for me alone, always meant for the benefit of the whole.

While some can see easily the miracle of everyday life, my mind seeks the causes of. As a child, sometimes told 'curiosity kills the cat' when I would get burned, physically or mentally rebuked, in some way for my curiosity of wanting to know the how's, the why's!

Without Spiritual signs, only working in faith we can easily lose hope, find ourselves living mostly in a physical "shell", where we feel spiritually alone, then we tend to look for human comfort, but that will only be a temporary fix.

God is the only ultimate filling up in our DNA, but a created planted need for that wholeness of God, deep in our souls.

To have a Good Godly faith, is better than to have just the hope! Yet it is both for believing, to feel Blessed Within!

Especially when it comes to the many mysteries of Spiritual knowledge it is in God's best time not ours to know.

Faith can be an act of power in itself, for either good or evil, so, equally important just what it is you are putting your faith in? For Good or less?
A lack of certainty works both ways in faith, and in doubting, ultimately some degree of just plain holding on to faith, at least the Hope. In both Job's Daughters and The Rosary, we start with Hope, Faith, and Love. "Charity" being the highest form of Love".

Even in times when there is no answer it is essential to find eventually true answers. Always in God's time.

Doesn't mean you can't ask and keep asking in faith until you can get one, but it can mean no, or not yet!

There are chemicals and electrical brain stimulations that are capable of producing out of the normal, extra-ordinary experiences by opening up the gates into the spiritual world, but such shortcuts are rarely recommended, as they pose personal psychological dangers. Such as those playing with Ouija boards, or just by thinking too many negative thoughts.

Lots of ways to open up a pathway to a negative spirit or experiences you may later regret having caused.

It is only with your own free will you learn to seek Holy Spirit Guidance or Confirmation, to find out whether you are on the right track or not.

The fruits of experience with the spiritual world for anyone, must be judged to be good or bad, not just for the individual, but equally as well, for the whole?

This may or may not be judged by one, or in one generation correctly, often in the past it has not been. Depending on its importance to history. I think learning to live together as a human family is our number one lesson for our generation of us older elders, as well as hoping to pass on to the youth our enduring strength, the possible good future in this life and the next, as faith tends to grow with time and experience, or it will tend to shrink into little or even nothing at all if we shy away from a Godly experience, the feeling of closeness with A Divine and unconditional Love.

"We live by faith not sight." 2 Cor. 5:7

"No one can see God"? What is really literally meant is we see only in part, like I could only see the top half of Jesus, who is so all alive in Spirit. But according to our physical mind's spiritual limitations I needed only to see the top half.

Not being able to see the fullness of God is why so many paintings and other forms of art are usually set in the cultural times they were created in, with clothes and facial features of that artist time. Often because the Patron or payer of the Artist was a richer Caucasian, it was painted in a paler tone in the Western World. In the east a little darker.

In our patriarchal times most often in masculine forms or described by masculine terms. God has the ability or means to choose to appear in any form, best presence in Spirit form in your heart!

Down through our knowable history people have reported to see what they believed to be visitors from "The Skies", some who even claim to be from other planets.

Ancient writings, as in India, tell of advanced civilizations being destroyed by means of advanced kinds of destruction even for our own day.

Usually because of a leader's excessive and immoral greed for power, selfishness, much like we face in our world now.

Since our planet is known to be millions of years old, in the past there may have been many civilizations, who became too greedy, uncaring and seemed to cause their own destruction, as much of our world seems now to be on the verge of doing?

Yet many of our ways, or traditions, have evolved gradually over time for the better, such as the amount of slavery, racism and sexism, and other forms of inequality. We've come a long way in making them better! Yet we still have a long way to go!

PREFERED MEMORIAL IMMORTALITY

When I am gone, no longer visibly around, do not look for me among the dead, for I am living on! If not, then not for me to know.

There or here on a bird's wing, or on a mountain top, just always want to be in the Heart of God.

No longer tied to one short time or space, like an ant or bee searching in this some-times incomprehensible world, for now just another spark of love, in the Heart of God, our Heaven here, and there. With Love, Grandma BC.

~

Watched a great movie "POMS" with Diana Keeton where they showed ashes being sent off in a 4th of July celebration fireworks. Spectacular, but didn't seem very sanitary, just back to the earth from where our physical bodies are seems best for me just as in "ashes to ashes, and dust to dust"!

Another must see movie by the great comedian of our times George Burns in "OH GOD"!

GOD AS THE BREATH OF LIFE
Boundless without end, God can be known as an Infinite Freeing of …
LOVE, PEACE, and JOY.
A GOD who is 'Not a god of partiality'.
God as One, infinite yet can Be Alive in each heart.

Trying to break free from my own cultural conditioned kind of thinking, to be able to express more of God's way of "Equality" thinking. Knowing words can be so easily misunderstood. Partly by where our hearts or motives are, but also from where our morality comes from.

Slavery, Sexism, all kinds of inequality, have been the morality of many, most of the Dictators Patriarchs, as well as good things they may have helped to create!

One of the reasons Humility is so important, when seeking Holiness is it comes from a word that means Our Wholeness. A way of seeing, and understanding, even sympathizing with how we all sin or fall short daily, by what we do or fail to do and yet each are still equally loved, while we are here to learn the ways!

If we each can sin in our seemingly being self-righteous, how can we think we are any better than others? Or for that matter much worse, than any other? Especially if we had to 'walk in their shoes' as the saying goes!

Humility is partly recognizing the Equality we do share with each other being created in God's Image!

It is Pride, a big source of inequality said to be the first sin from the evil one, and our own, that wants us to put our individual selves on a pedestal or to put others below us in inferior positions, to assert our will, to have our own selfish way. Sometimes to make our-selves feel better. At the expense of others. Pride will rear its head when we are only considering Self, leaving out the Other.

We experience the opposite when we ourselves have been put down too often as not being thought of as enough, then we can have a lack of self-worth or very little self-confidence that tends to make us think others are so much better! We then tend to put others on a pedestal and negate ourselves, to the point of harm to both.

Another form of pride is thinking we deserve more than others. We see or feel we have been favored or have more in some way such as talents, good looks, or money, and have yet to know as Jesus and others have warned: those given much, much more is expected from them.

Best to see our reality from an unselfish way, not how we might sometimes feel like Lording it over others; or shy away from doing what we can, when or where needed.

Selfishness and greed can make it seem justified to take more than what we need or not want to share fairly with others, leaving us later to face the misery and consequences of such decisions and actions, that have done harm to others, as well as to our own souls.

Very hard to break habits of this kind of thinking we may have learned from the way we have been treated by those who may or may not have been able to love, or at least seemed at the time not to care very much about us.

Yet as we keep evolving, growing in knowledge and spiritual maturity, we can't help but become aware of our own "Equality". For it is a God given right of Freedom that is written into most people's normal nature to want, even cherish those Equal Human Rights that stop only at the Equal Rights of others.

We have been evolving into the understanding, if not always the practice of The Golden Rule, as a Universal belief standard, found in the hearts of most good people, and we are at our best, when we put it into practice for the benefit of All. By our cooperating and working with each other, rather than in endless competitive conflicts ending even in wars between peoples and nations, races and belief systems.

Only for very special reasons at special times, for the good of all, does God miraculously set aside the usual laws of nature, as they normally are meant to apply for all equally. We need such a miracle in our time for an opening of the rainbows pot of Gold. To be shared equally!

The Equalitarian Age, a culture based on Equal Rights and Equal Opportunity for all, according to their talents, abilities, desire, seems to be our next best step into evolving into the best that our human natures can be!

To start with, a world-wide fair minimum wage, that would help us go into Peace. Knowing if we do not take the necessary steps towards Peace settlements we will surely soon again be going into more war and destruction!

Prophecy given to us to warn, to encourage, to give hope for better outcomes, as we choose now either probably nuclear war or a long time of Peace, prosperity, happiness and Joys.

You may think changing to "Equality" to achieve those things would be too hard. You need the Belief that nothing is too hard to do, as you will be given the strength, when God is working with you and others!

You may think there is no way out of the systems, of the top down pyramid type of inequality overall, that has for so long overridden or hidden the Equal Rights of all, even among the universal Golden Rule message in all major Scriptures.

You may even feel like many, wanting to head for some Caribbean Island, that is until a Sonoma wave sinks it, as our Islands will eventually sink with rising tides of not doing anything or enough, about Climate Change, we have greatly been contributing to, without going Green, in using Wind and Solar. Rebuilding electrical and crumbling infrastructure, would provide good paying jobs for years. Few know how to go back to living without electricity, gardens, canning, smoke houses, outside outhouses, and fresh water

There are no underground cities that would last long, not even caves safer any more than they were in Cave man times.

Why shouldn't we at least try to reason this out together? Even with those who do not want to consider the possibility or belief in an after this life, life. You at least want to prolong life in the best way possible for as long as possible. The privilege's we enjoy in the best of modern civilizations that are still possible.

Forming better relationships means being aware of the possible why's for other's negative feelings, as well as our own, usually some form of fears, envy, past hurts. Misunderstood scriptural beliefs, ego or power tripping, even attempts to impose negative traditions or customs.

Don't let other people's negative feelings keep you from being free to be objective, to act in ways that control your own as well as others negative actions in a non-violent way. Working to help co-create Peace, comes first from God's spiritual renewal!

Have felt so strongly God's Presence, only three times in my life, and to hear only One Word of Prophecy during the second time "Equality" in experiencing God's Presence.

When I finally asked for a Spiritual "Rebirth", out of a need to experience God again, knowing from Jesus teachings we each one when we are ready or receptive, need to be "reborn". * John 3:3-8

I had lots of doubts in my late youth, and young adulthood about being able to believe in a God who did not seem fair or just, like many historical worshipped gods! Appearing god-like to primitive people here, if from another planet.

Each of us need a spiritual rebirth. To be able to know, experience for ourself our own Creator God who is Loving.

To be able to recognize that Holy voice within, apart from your own voice, or others. For some spirits, not so good, will try to lead you to become very selfish even to be a bully and hurtful to others. While rationalizing to yourself you have the right or to think you have the power of that spirit. The higher Spirit or God will not tell you to hurt others. Regardless of what men's words tell you, even if in scriptures. Or if that is the way you have been treated and want revenge. Do not repeat the evil. Important to break those cycles of hurt and destruction if that is your situation, for your sake as well as others. By fruits of Goodness, your spiritual source is known. You will need to Judge by your good or bad fruits, by the results of what you are being led to do.

Only God's Holy Spirit can give you a Blessing of Peace and Joy that will well up within you.

Worldly sought pleasures are always temporary, fleeting, like 'here today and gone tomorrow'. Not so with God's Holy Spirit, can stay with you forever, but only if you want, it will also leave if you really no longer want to care or believe.

Still, while you are here on earth, it will remain near, even when not wanted, like any Loving Parent would if it could. God Can! Once asked for, will continue to wait for your need usually for most, near the end of life or when you've had enough pain and misery from following after the many false gods there are in this world.

THE BEST TO KEEP YOUR HOPE, FOR IS HOPE NOT BETTER THAN NONE!

P.S. I believe God's Hand was shown to me, as to other Prophets of God mostly for my own sign, so I would know to warn of what I had experienced to an even worse World War III at this time, if we don't go towards "Equality". Those who have had God's "Rebirth", as well as those who want more of Blessings Within.

Maybe you have felt the danger of war near us too, if you can remember World War II, or have lived through any war since? Will know we are closer than ever, to a thermonuclear or nuclear World War, that could put the whole world back into the dark ages. Months without the Sun getting through the dark clouds. Years or centuries without uncontaminated water or food.

How Biblically typical of God to confront the power of Hitler's kind of fascism, military might and Inequality by appearing to a small, insignificant little 5yr. old. I am so thankful for waiting till I sat down, knowing such a sight has literally knocked grown men off their feet! In my being so young, would never be tempted to think it was from any special merit of my own, that I had earned. If anything, it was the great faith my parents had in God, passed on at that time in me as their first beloved child. How true the Catholic saying that 'Families that pray together stay together'!

We now have several such men in charge of even much more military might than in Hitler's time, who seem to have some maybe even less of a sense of morality or an honest nature? Without trusting in God's Power more than evil in positions of power to help us now, who else would be able to do much to prevent them?

Praise be to the Military Elders who have seen enough of such evil and unnecessary destruction. I believe they are here at this time of our need and need to Pray they continue to have that power but let us keep only Good People in all levels of governing us. They will only be as good as voters are!

With so much inequality in our world only a matter of time many feel as our pot of world tensions continues to boil higher. Like in the boiling of country frog's legs, on a hot stove. We like them will need courage to jump out, to get out of the such a pot, afraid of being caught by earthly monsters'! Yet we are not frogs!

The knowledge of what is possible is given for our times to help prevent a World War III! I believe we were allowed this viral plague instead of the nuclear war I was thinking we were close to, to help stop us in our tracks and access where we are, what it is we value most about life, our specific lives at this time. But that we each must decide, hopefully by confirming for yourself with God, as to what if anything you might be able to do besides pray, what you can do with the help of others to prevent a war at least not in any time in the near future!

If you don't decide to confirm, or allow God's Holy Spirit to live within you, to experience for yourself a spiritual rebirth, then may God have mercy on your soul, as it may also have been the only reason you were given a soul or consciousness, in this short taste of eternal life, by your Creator. For how Can I, or anyone prove you are a spiritual Soul or Spirit, as well as Physical Being?

No, just as you can't either disprove it. No one at this time can prove God exist or the opposite that there is no God! Only by experiencing for yourself.

Experience the Divine as a Living, Loving Being, is what brings most people happiness, even under adverse living situations. Best to at least try to make contact with such a love for yourself and others, if you are not already sure.

If you are not free of sin or not want to have a "spiritual rebirth" then hopefully you will be able to confirm or accept the evidence found in Universal "Golden Rule" as a fast way to help everyone's equal rights by stop supporting inequality or discrimination for the female half to help in rebalancing our world to one of "Equality"!

But what to do when it is your Boss, your Pastor, your husband, or your Wife, Your Teacher? The list goes on and on, we are so intrinsically entwined, at this late date in our so called "civilized" history!

It may be our primary purpose or example, for those of you who have made it, creating the best kind of life when we are willing to go towards The Better Will, rather than our own more selfish limiting view!

My own lack of faith at one point in my life resulted in the lowest point until I felt I needed to know with more certainty, after nine years of maybe it was all just a matter of mindful illusions. "Well I am all prayed up" were my thoughts after two weeks, I can no longer fast or pray anymore, "so I guess there really is no God", as I sat in my comfortable living room chair, "or surely I would have had some kind of a sign by now". It wasn't till then, like a silent but a mighty wind I felt God's Holy Spirit come through the outside walls of my living room where I sat, to completely fill up the whole room, wash away all doubts, then to hear clearly only the one resounding distinct word of "EQUALITY".

Would then realize it had been me all along who had turned away from being willing to trust, how the good man Job had trusted, in Job 1:20 "God Gives, God Takes Away, Blessed Be the Name of God."

If I can leave you with but one favorite verse it would have to be: "God is Love, and when we love, we live in God and God lives in us." I John 4:16

For Blessings Within as well as without!

UNIVERSAL GOLDEN RULES

"Hurt not others in ways that you yourself would find hurtful." Buddhism: Udana-Varga 5,1

"All things whatsoever ye would that men should do to you, do ye so to them; for this is the law and the prophets." Christianity: Matthew 7:12

"Do not do to others what you would not like for yourself. Then there will be no resentment against you, either in the family or in the state." Confucianism: Analects 12:2

"This is the sum of duty; do naught onto others what you would not have them do unto you." Hinduism: Mahabharata 5,1517

"No one of you is a believer until he desires for his brother that which he desires for himself." Islam: Sunnah

"What is hateful to you, do not do to your fellowman. This is the Law; all the rest is commentary." Judaism: Talmud, Shabbat 3id

"Regard your neighbor's gain as your gain, and your neighbor's loss as your own loss." Taoism: Tai Shang Kan Yin P'ien

"That nature is good which refrains from doing to another whatsoever is not good for itself." Zoroastrianism: Dadaistic-I-deink, 94,5

HOLY SPIRIT PRAYER

HOLY SPIRIT GUIDE ME TO KNOW WHAT IS
BEST TO DO
I WILL LISTEN TO YOU
FOR YOU ARE THE BEST WITHIN ME
LEADING ME TO THE FULLNESS OF TRUTH
WHEN I AM WILLING TO FOLLOW YOU

I WILL ACCEPT ALL THAT YOU PERMIT
THE PAIN AS WELL AS THE SUNSHINE
AS THE BEST WAY TO GROW SPIRITUALLY
FOR THE SAKE OF MY SOUL

DAILY I WILL SEEK YOUR PERFECT WILL
FOR MYSELF AND EQUALLY FOR OTHERS

International Library of Poetry
Award from Poetry.com

BESSED WITHIN-A Prophecy of Equality

In translating scriptures into the present day patriarchal languages, only the Father Image was used, with male nouns, pronouns tending to create a false image of God, the sin of idolatry! Earliest Priestly stories say: male and female both created in the Image of God. In Genesis 1:27; and in 5:1.

The Holy Spirit spoke to The Church Bishops "to end the discrimination of racism, sex…as not the Will of God". Article 29 Pastoral Constitution of Vatican II in 1965.

Pointing to inequality being the root cause of war and poverty.

As the Universal Message of The Golden Rule found in Good Hearts. With Equal Rights the more cooperative females could help balance, negotiate, bargain, with more aggressive male natures, to avoid more, now near, nuclear wars.

There is a God of Equality! If free from male/idolatry can Confirm with The Holy Spirit, who guides to the fullness of Truth. Help stop inequality, share this Prophecy, especially with Pope Francis, Vatican City, Rome, Italy 00120 to help end discrimination for the female half.

For Blessings, www.equality4peace.org

"2 MIRACLES 4 PEACE"
Free at website in 4 sections
www.equality4peace.org

"GOD ANSWERED "EQUALITY"
ISBN-13:987-1490328348

"EQUAL RIGHTS FROM GOD" or "THE EQUALITARIAN AGE
www.amazon.com/dp/151148148x

Bible verses taken from The Zondervan Parallel New Testament in Greek and English and International Version 1990 in Grand Rapids, Michigan 49530 USA. All those in agreement with the corresponding Catholic verses.

Many Sources sought for the originals include, The Aramaic Monastery, in the Old City in Jerusalem, holds the original meanings of the Aramaic common language of the People in Jesus time.

Thank You for reading, sharing or leaving a comment.
equality4peace@yahoo.com or "BLESSED WITHIN" www.amazon.com/dp/1689926341
You will remain in my prayers for Peace and Blessings.

Printed in the United States
By Bookmasters